THE FISCAL IMPACT OF RESIDENTIAL AND COMMERCIAL DEVELOPMENT: A Case Study

Thomas Muller
Grace Dawson

712-7-1 December 1972

THE URBAN INSTITUTE
WASHINGTON, D.C.

The research and studies forming the basis for this publication were conducted with financial support of the Ford Foundation. The views expressed are those of the authors and do not necessarily represent the views of the sponsor of the research or of The Urban Institute.

REFER TO URI-22000 WHEN ORDERING.

ISBN 87766-074-3

UI 712-7-1

Available from

Publications Office
The Urban Institute
2100 M Street, N.W.
Washington, D.C. 20037

List price: $3.00

C/74/1500

ABSTRACT

This paper suggests a method for estimating the difference between revenues to be received by a county government from a proposed residential and non-residential development and expenditures to be incurred by the county as a result of the development.

The introductory section of the paper provides a general overview of the methods used to estimate the difference, and also discusses some of the reasons such estimates are useful to local government officials in making sound land-use decisions.

In Chapters One through Six, and the related Appendices, the general methods are applied to a proposed development consisting of approximately 800 residential units and 30 acres of commercial development in Albemarle County, Virginia, a rapidly growing area surrounding the city of Charlottesville. Detailed revenue and expenditure data associated with this development are presented, and in an appendix the fiscal impact the development is likely to have on the State of Virginia is also estimated.

The results of this revenue-expenditure analysis indicate that total County expenditures associated with the proposed development will exceed County revenues from the development by an annual amount of $101,745 (given 30-year bond repayment periods for capital outlays). In the final chapter a number of policy alternatives are suggested for offsetting this negative fiscal effect on the County. These include requiring the developer to compensate the County for the deficit or obliging him to choose an alternative location within the County where public facilities may be underutilized.

PREFACE

The Public Interest Research Project of The Urban Institute conducts studies in a number of fields where the expertise and skills of Institute staff coincide with issues in current or prospective litigation or administrative proceedings. This paper on the fiscal impact of new development represents one such effort. Earlier papers in this series are:

1. "The Validity and Discriminatory Impact of the Federal Service Entrance Examination," by Robert Sadacca, assisted by Joan Brackett;

2. "Inequality in Local Government Services: A Case Study of Neighborhood Roads," by Andrew J. Boots, III, Grace Dawson, William Silverman and Harry P. Hatry; and

3. "Residential Zoning and Equal Housing Opportunities: A Case Study in Black Jack, Missouri," by Ronald F. Kirby, Frank deLeeuw, and William Silverman, with the assistance of Grace Dawson.

Topics for studies are suggested by public officials, lawyers, or interested Institute staff members. Regardless of the source of a research issue, all resulting publications represent the objective and policy-oriented approach of The Urban Institute. The findings and conclusions of the studies are made available to judges, administrators, lawyers, and to the general public.

Thomas Muller of the Institute's senior research staff developed the methodology for this study and Grace Dawson of the Public Interest Research Project participated in the organization, writing, and editing of the study. I should also like to acknowledge the invaluable secretarial support of Susan Carey.

William Silverman
Director of the
Public Interest Research Project

TABLE OF CONTENTS

ABSTRACT iii

PREFACE v

INTRODUCTION 1

- The Need for Fiscal Impact Studies 1
- Outline of Methodology 2
  - Background Profiles 2
  - Revenue Estimates 4
  - Operating Expenditure Estimates 8
  - Capital Expenditure Estimates 11
  - Net Fiscal Effect 12
- A General Guide to the Study and Its Application 13

CHAPTER ONE. BACKGROUND OF ALBEMARLE COUNTY 15

- Demographic and Socioeconomic Characteristics 17
  - Population and Demography 17
  - Income 19
  - Cost of Housing 20
  - Impact of the University of Virginia 21

CHAPTER TWO. REVENUE AND EXPENDITURE TRENDS IN ALBEMARLE COUNTY 23

- Local Revenues 23
- Local Operating Expenditures 26
- Local Capital Expenditures 29

CHAPTER THREE. REVENUE ESTIMATES: HOLLYMEAD PHASE I 31

Households 31

Real Property Taxes 33

Personal Property and Sales Taxes 34

Other Taxes 38

Household Revenue Summary 40

Business Enterprises 40

Real Property Taxes from Existing Land Use 43

Federal Revenue Sharing 43

CHAPTER FOUR. OPERATING EXPENDITURE ESTIMATES: HOLLYMEAD PHASE I 45

General Methodology 45

Allocation of Operating Expenditures for Services Used By Households 49

Education 49

Non-Education Operating Expenditures 53

Total Operating Expenditures Allocated to Households 59

Allocation of Operating Expenditures for Services Used By Business Enterprises 60

CHAPTER FIVE. CAPITAL EXPENDITURE ESTIMATES: HOLLYMEAD PHASE I 63

General Methodology 63

Long-Term Debt Vs. Pay-As-You-Build Financing 64

The Useful Economic Life of the Investment 66

Economies and Diseconomies of Scale 67

Capital Expenditures Allocated to Households in Hollymead Phase I 68

Education 68

Recreation 71

Government Services Substation 72

Landfill Site 73

Hospitals 73

Total Capital Costs Per Household 74

Capital Expenditures Allocated to Existing and New Households in the County 74

Capital Expenditures Financed From Current Revenues 75

Capital Expenditures Financed From Current Revenue and General Obligation Bonds 77

Capital Expenditures Allocated to Business Enterprises 79

Capital Expenditures Allocated to Hollymead Phase I Business Enterprises 79

Capital Expenditures Allocated to Existing and New County Business Enterprises 79

CHAPTER SIX. FINDINGS AND POLICY ALTERNATIVES 81

Revenue-Expenditure Summary 81

Revenues 81

Operating Expenditures 81

Capital Expenditures Linked to Hollymead Phase I 81

Capital Expenditures Associated with the Entire County 85

Fiscal Flow Summary 86

Findings 87

Policy Alternatives 89

APPENDIX A. SELECTED DEMOGRAPHIC AND SOCIOECONOMIC CHARACTERISTICS OF NEW COMMUNITIES WITHIN ALBEMARLE COUNTY 91

APPENDIX B. THE IMPACT OF THE HOLLYMEAD DEVELOPMENT ON THE STATE GOVERNMENT 97

APPENDIX C. THE NET FISCAL IMPACT OF THE ENTIRE NORTH RIVANNA COMMUNITY CLUSTER ON ALBEMARLE COUNTY 119

APPENDIX D. ESTIMATION OF EXPECTED SCHOOL ENROLLMENT BASED ON FERTILITY PROJECTIONS 125

APPENDIX E. ESTIMATION OF CAPITAL EXPENDITURES BASED ON THE COUNTY'S PROJECTED CAPITAL IMPROVEMENT PROGRAM 127

APPENDIX F. ADDITIONAL FACTORS TO BE EXAMINED 129

APPENDIX G. DATA SOURCES FOR A FISCAL IMPACT ANALYSIS 133

LIST OF TABLES

1. 1964-1972 Change in Albemarle County Revenue 24
2. 1964-1972 Change in Albemarle County Assessed Property Value 25
3. Albemarle County-Funded Operating Expenditures 27
4. Residential Density for Dwellings in Hollymead Phase I 31
5. Annual Real Property Tax for Hollymead Phase I 33
6. Ratio of House Value to Annual Household Income for Hollymead Phase I 34
7. Personal Property Tax Per Household in Hollymead Phase I 36
8. Redistribution of State Sales Tax Revenue Per Household in Hollymead Phase I 37
9. County Sales Tax Revenues Per Household in Hollymead Phase I 38
10. Utility Taxes Per Household in Hollymead Phase I 39
11. Distribution of ABC Tax Revenue Per Household in Hollymead Phase I 40
12. Total Annual County Revenues From Households in Hollymead Phase I 41
13. Annual County Revenues From Commercial Development in Hollymead Phase I 42
14. Real Property Base in Albemarle County by Land-Use Type--Fiscal 1972 47
15. Allocation of Operating Expenditures for Services Used by Business Enterprises and Households in Albemarle County 48
16. Determination of Operating Expenditures Per Student (ADM) for Education in Albemarle County 51
17. Operating Expenditures Per Student for Education in Hollymead Phase I 52

18. The Impact of the State Sales Tax Redistribution 53

19. Allocation of Non-Education Operating Expenditures to Hollymead Phase I Households on the Basis of Household Income 58

20. Allocation of Non-Education Operating Expenditures to Hollymead Phase I Households on a Per Capita Basis 59

21. Allocation of Operating Expenditures to Hollymead Phase I Households: Summary 59

22. Operating Expenditures Allocated to Business Enterprises 61

23. Fiscal 1972 Capital Expenditures Per Student--Albemarle County As Compared with Fairfax County 69

24. Capital Expenditures Per Student in Hollymead Phase I 70

25. Capital Expenditures for Recreation--Hollymead Phase I 71

26. Capital Expenditures for Governmental Services Substation--Hollymead Phase I 72

27. Capital Expenditures for Landfill--Hollymead Phase I 73

28. Capital Expenditures--Households in Hollymead Phase I 74

29. Albemarle County Capital Expenditures, Fiscal 1972 76

30. Allocation of Capital Expenditures to Households in Hollymead Phase I Financed from Current Revenues 77

31. Allocation of Capital Expenditures Financed from Current Revenue and General Obligation Bonds to Households in Hollymead Phase I 78

32. Allocation of Capital Expenditures to Business Enterprises in Hollymead Phase I 79

33. Allocation of Capital Expenditures to New and Existing Business Enterprises 80

34. Hollymead Phase I: Total Annual Revenue-Expenditure Summary 83

35. Net Deficit Per Annum for Dwelling Units in Hollymead Phase I 86

A-1. Family Income Distribution by District 92

A-2. Distribution of House Value for Owner-Occupied Units 93

A-3. Distribution of Public and Private School Students by District 94

B-1. State Revenues--General Fund (1971-1972) 97

B-2. State Income Tax Payments--Hollymead Phase I Households 99

B-3. State Sales Tax Collections--Hollymead Phase I Households 100

B-4. Total State Revenues from Households in Hollymead Phase I 101

B-5. General Fund Appropriations, 1971-1972 (Categorical Grants) 104

B-6. State Aid for Public Education--Hollymead Phase I Households 106

B-7. Non-Education Direct State Aid to Albemarle County 108

B-8. Total Direct State Aid to Albemarle County--Hollymead Phase I Households 108

B-9. Indirect State Aid to Albemarle County--Hollymead Phase I Households 112

B-10. Estimated Car Trips--Hollymead Phase I Households 114

B-11. Total Direct and Indirect State Grants--Hollymead Phase I Households 115

B-12. Total Direct and Indirect State Grants--Hollymead Phase I Business Enterprises 115

B-13. Hollymead Phase I--Total State Revenues and Expenditures 116

C-1. Total Albemarle County Annual Revenues from Households and Business Enterprises in the North Rivanna Community Cluster 121

C-2. Total Albemarle County Annual Operating and Capital Expenditures for Households and Business Enterprises in the North Rivanna Community Cluster 122

C-3. North Rivanna Community Cluster--Total Annual County Revenue-Expenditure Summary 123

E-1. Proposed Capital Projects for Albemarle County 127

INTRODUCTION

THE NEED FOR FISCAL IMPACT STUDIES

The fiscal impact of residential and commercial development on the local public sector has been the subject of considerable discussion and recent litigation.[1] Measuring the difference between expected revenues from proposed development and anticipated expenditures incurred as a result of growth has become increasingly important as the nation's metropolitan areas continue to expand.

Suburbs, in which a large share of national growth has taken place, are particularly concerned that the cost of providing public services to new residents may contribute to rapid property tax rate increases and/or deterioration in the level and quality of public services. During the last decade the national population increased by 23.8 million. Of this total, suburbs accounted for 80 percent of the growth, central cities less than 3 percent, while rural areas lost population.[2]

Unfortunately, objective analyses of the fiscal impact of growth have been scarce. This study presents a general methodology for evaluating the fiscal effect on a county of proposed residential and non-residential development which can also be applied to other political jurisdictions with appropriate

---

1. For example, Golden v. Planning Board, N.Y. Ct. App., 5/3/72, cert. denied, ___ U.S. ___, 41 LW 3268, 11/14/72; and Lee Jackson Development Corporation and Levitt and Sons, Inc. v. The Board of Supervisors of Loudoun County, Va., Cir. Ct. Loudoun Cty., Va., 3/22/72.

2. For a discussion of government policies which influence growth patterns, see Executive Office of The President, Report on National Growth--1972, Washington, D.C., 1972.

adjustments. It should be noted that while the net fiscal effect of development should be taken into account in land-use decisions, it is only one of a number of issues which should be examined. The impact of new development on the physical and social environment, as well as on the private sector of the economy, should also be considered. In addition, the equity issues raised by the existing tax structure, the secondary fiscal effect of non-residential development,[3] and the current distribution of public services should also be weighed. Because these are complex issues and beyond the purpose of this study, they will not be examined.

This study consists of two major parts. The introductory section presents a general framework for evaluating county revenues and expenditures associated with proposed residential and non-residential development and discusses how this framework can be used. Chapters one through six and the Appendices contain a fiscal impact case study--an evaluation of the proposed Hollymead development in Albemarle County, Virginia.

OUTLINE OF METHODOLOGY

<u>BACKGROUND PROFILES</u> (See Chapters One and Two)[4]

Prior to undertaking the actual revenue-expenditure analysis of a proposed development project, it is useful to compile two county profiles.

First, a general profile of changes in the social and economic characteristics of the county over the past decade should be made. This should include the following items:

---

3. The secondary fiscal effect occurs as follows: commercial development increases the demand for housing, thereby inducing residential development which in turn increases the demand for goods and services.

4. Major subsections in the Introduction refer the reader to the corresponding portions of the Albemarle County case study.

Population and Demography. What is the county population, growth rate, rate of mobility, fertility rate, etc.? Are these rates increasing or decreasing?

Income of County Residents. What is the median family income of the county as compared with the state and other counties of similar character? At what rate has it been increasing or decreasing?

Cost of Housing. What is the median cost of different types of housing in the county as compared with similar types of housing throughout the state and in other similar counties? Is housing primarily renter or owner occupied?

Special Group Impact. Does any population sub-group exist in abnormal proportion in the county? Does this sub-group have an impact on the fiscal structure of the county? (E.g., a large student population may affect the cost of housing or wage rates, or a large elderly population may result in reduced education expenditures and increased health and special transportation costs.)

The second general profile should examine the changes in the county's fiscal structure over a previous period of growth. The following items should be considered:

Changes in Local Revenue. What are the basic sources of local revenue? What new sources (new sales taxes, utility taxes, etc.) have been added during the growth period? What is the amount of total local revenue derived from households and business enterprises, and at what rate have revenues increased?

Changes in Local Expenditures. At what rate have total population and number of school children increased, implying increased capital costs for education? What wage increases have occurred? What changes have occurred in the general level and quality of public services? Has the increased population created the demand for new and expanded public services? Has the share of the budget allocated for capital expenditures and debt service remained relatively constant?

The analysis of the fiscal impact of a specific proposed residential and/or non-residential development falls under three major headings. Estimates should be computed of: (1) revenues from the development: (2) operating expenditures incurred by the development; and (3) capital expenditures incurred by the development.

REVENUE ESTIMATES (See Chapter Three)

Local revenue can be grouped into four categories: (1) revenues associated with property wealth (which in most jurisdictions represents the largest revenue source); (2) revenues associated with income and level of consumption, which is comprised primarily of local sales and utility taxes; (3) per capita revenues, which are derived from either a per capita tax or total population; and (4) miscellaneous revenues, which include fees, fines, licenses, and other minor items.[5]

REVENUES RELATED TO PROPERTY

Both real and personal property are generally taxed at the local level, however, in several states, including New York and Delaware, only real property is taxed. In general, the same tax rate applies to both residential

5. For the purposes of analysis, revenues from business enterprises should be identified separately from revenues collected from households. It is also useful, when proposed residential development includes different types of housing units, to estimate revenues (and expenditures) for each type of unit such as single family, townhouse, apartment.

and non-residential property.[6] In many jurisdictions, income producing property, including apartments, is taxed on the basis of gross or net income, rather than on the basis of the value of property.

In almost all communities, the effective tax rate is lower than the assessed tax rate. Therefore, in computing likely revenues from real property, one has to determine the effective tax rate based on recent property sales. Frequently, it is assumed that the "adjusted" tax rate, which is in theory the rate applied to property, yields an estimate of likely taxes from real property. However, because of the time lag in assessment, as well as other factors, the adjusted tax rate is, with few exceptions, higher than the effective tax rate.[7]

In about fifteen states, such as Maryland, Virginia, and North Carolina, school districts are fiscally dependent as part of the local budget. In other states, school districts can levy their own property tax independently of other political jurisdictions.[8]

Property taxes on personal property of households are most frequently on automobiles, and, in some areas, on household goods. Business personal property taxes may include taxes on machinery and inventory.

REVENUES RELATED TO INCOME

Revenues linked to income include local sales and income taxes, utility taxes (insofar as higher income households consume utilities more intensively) and occasionally excise taxes on specific goods. In general, however, taxes

---

6. There are exceptions to this, including Minnesota which taxes industrial and commercial property at a higher rate than residential property.

7. In evaluating new development, the likely market value of land and structures is usually provided by the developer. The values can be compared to similar property to determine if they reasonably reflect the local market.

8. For school district revenue by source of funding, see B. Levin, T. Muller, and W. Scanlon, Public School Finance: Present Disparities and Fiscal Alternatives (Washington, D.C.: The Urban Institute, 1972).

on beer, alcoholic beverages, gasoline, cigarettes, and related items are not subject to county taxes. Gift and estate taxes related to wealth are generally the prerogative of state and federal governments.

In view of the importance of income-related taxes in many jurisdictions, it is necessary to estimate the likely household income of new residents. One approach for estimating the income of potential residents, based on the relationship between property value and income, is discussed in the Albemarle County case study.[9] If monthly rent payments for apartment units are known, annual rents can be computed and income estimates can be derived by taking rent payments as a share of income.[10] It should be noted that the type of housing (owner-occupied or rented) as well as the share of income allocated for each type of housing varies by location, age, race, and size of the household.

A more direct method for estimating income of new residents is to examine applications to mortgage institutions, and apartment managers. However, access to these data is difficult because of confidentiality. Given data on income, likely receipts from various sales and excise taxes can be approximated from various surveys on expenditures by income class, region, and metropolitan area.[11]

---

9. See p. 34. For a discussion of the demand for housing as a function of income, see F. deLeeuw, "The Demand for Housing: A Review of Cross Section Evidence," The Review of Economies and Statistics, Vol. 53, February 1971, pp. 1-10.

10. A number of government publications discuss these proportions. For example, see U.S. Department of Labor, Three Standards of Living for Urban Families, Bulletin No. 1570-5, 1969.

11. U.S. Department of Labor, Bureau of Labor Statistics, Survey of Consumer Expenditures, Report No. 237-88 (Washington, D.C.: U.S. Government Printing Office, 1965).

PER CAPITA REVENUE

Local government occasionally, as in parts of Delaware, administers a per capita, or "head" tax on all adults. More frequently, local government is the recipient of state or county revenues distributed on the basis of the number of residents or the number of students. For example, profits from the alcoholic beverage sales by the state are distributed to local jurisdictions in Virginia based on population. As a result, per capita revenues vary in proportion to changes in population. Federal revenue sharing for local jurisdictions as presently legislated, uses population as one criterion.[12]

MISCELLANEOUS REVENUE

Other sources of revenue, such as automobile license tags, can also be estimated on the basis of income (higher income households tend to have more cars per dwelling unit compared to lower income households). Fines and other minor sources can be approximated on the basis of per capita receipts from these sources by the jurisdiction.

Local revenue sources may vary within states. Among states there are considerable tax structure differences. Examples of local taxes not illustrated in the Albemarle County case study include taxes on payrolls and state income tax surtaxes. Both of these taxes, however, can be estimated utilizing the methodology suggested.

12. Per capita income and tax effort are the other criteria. As a result, affluent Fairfax County, Virginia, receives only $8.18 per capita while adjoining Loudoun County receives $16.01.

OPERATING EXPENDITURE[13] ESTIMATES (See Chapter Four)

The importance and scope of public services which are the responsibility of local government can differ sharply among and within states. In some communities, utilities such as water and sewerage are part of the municipal budget; certain roads and highways are built as well as maintained by many localities. In addition, while expenditures for health and welfare may be small items in some county budgets, they are major expenditure items in cities such as New York and Detroit.

Local operating expenditures can be grouped into (1) those incurred in supplying services used primarily by households, such as education, libraries, health and welfare, and recreation, and (2) those incurred in supplying services used by both business enterprises and households, such as fire and police services, utilities, and general government.

OPERATING EXPENDITURES RELATED TO HOUSEHOLDS

In most local jurisdictions, public education is the largest expenditure item. In suburban areas of states other than those which have large state funding for education, such as North Carolina and Delaware, education accounts for 40 to 80 percent of local current expenditures. As a result, a reliable estimate of additional school population resulting from development is a critical variable in estimating the fiscal impact of new development.[14] Factors which affect the number of students attending public schools include type of housing, demographic and socioeconomic characteristics of households, the availability of private and parochial schools,

---

13. In general it should be noted that throughout the expenditure sections of this study, costs incurred as a result of development are examined rather than benefits accrued.

14. In the Albemarle County case study, two techniques for estimating the likely number of students from new development are discussed.

value of new housing, and prior residence of new households in a community. The grade distribution of students is frequently a function of housing type, and since per student costs are higher in upper grades, the use of average per student cost values may be misleading.

In recent years, many communities have come to support junior colleges and other post-high school educational facilities. The demand for these facilities, which frequently have open enrollment policies, needs to be estimated, together with the likely demand for adult education.

Household related expenditures, other than education, can be categorized[15] according to whether:

<u>Demand is concentrated among low-income households</u>: e.g., public health services aimed at indigents and low-income households, and welfare services;

<u>Demand increases with income</u>: e.g., libraries, recreation, and waste collection;

<u>Demand increases with size of property or structure</u>: e.g., water, sewerage, storm drains, and road repavement; or

<u>Demand is generally invariable</u>: e.g., police, fire, and general government.

In the revenue expenditure analysis discussed in this paper, only demand for services which is most likely to result in increased spending

---

15. These categories are only general guides. For example, part of a county health budget serves the entire population independent of income. Library and recreation facility use increase with income, but may decline at very high incomes, where the public service is replaced by private facilities. High income households are likely to utilize private rather than public golf courses and tennis courts, and are likely to purchase books rather than borrow them from public libraries.

Certain crimes and the frequency of fires tend to increase in low-income areas. However, this does not necessarily result in a level of expenditures for public safety which reduces crime and fire incidence to a level comparable with more affluent areas of a jurisdiction.

is considered. The demand may exist for special expenditures for education or health care in low income areas, however, unless past trends indicate that this demand is likely to be met by additional spending, no potential expenditure will be considered in the calculation.

It should be recognized that increases in the demand for services, as a result of either small increases in population or change in taste, do not necessarily result in an immediate increase in expenditures. For example, five new households are not likely to result in an increase in public safety, recreation, or other public service personnel. Thus, costs that remain fixed for a small increment in demand, rise sharply as the demand reaches a critical point, and remain fixed until demand again reaches a threshold value. In the absence of data on these threshold values, costs can frequently be averaged, rather than attributing the total incremental cost to the marginal unit which triggered the additional expenditure. Changes in local spending which are attributable to changes in population should be distinguished from those attributable to other factors.[16]

OPERATING EXPENDITURES RELATED TO RESIDENTS AND BUSINESS ENTERPRISES

Public services used by both households and business enterprises include utilities, transportation facilities, police and fire protection, the judicial system, and general government functions. In many cases, it is difficult to isolate the household demand from that of commercial or industrial enterprises, such as special equipment for fighting industrial fires, or police

---

16. Whether unit costs of public services increase faster in an area of rapid development compared to areas with stable population requires further study. It has been shown that jurisdictions with rapid growth have higher property taxes, which could be attributable to one or more of the following factors: (1) the necessity for large capital outlays; (2) diseconomies of scale; and/or (3) rapidly increasing salaries for public employees.

patrols in industrial parks. Alternative techniques for allocating operating expenditures among enterprises and households can be based on level of employment in commercial and industrial facilities as compared to number of household units, or the ratio of the property value of such facilities to residential property value.

<u>CAPITAL EXPENDITURE ESTIMATES</u> (See Chapter Five)

Capital expenditures associated with new development include: (1) facilities linked directly with the proposed development, such as new schools, sewer lines, fire stations, and other new facilities; and (2) facilities to be constructed as part of a capital improvement plan which will be shared by existing residents or enterprises in the jurisdiction as well as those from the new development, such as junior colleges, new sewage and/or water treatment plants, and health care centers. Facilities in the second category are not usually triggered by a single new development project, but may be designed to incorporate increases in demand from projected development.

In order to determine whether a capital expenditure should be allocated to the existing residents exclusively or jointly to existing and new residents, the following questions should be answered:

- Would the facilities be built regardless of the approval of a proposed development?
- Would the proposed size of the facilities remain constant regardless of population increase resulting from new development?
- Would new residents be users, and thus beneficiaries, of the proposed facilities?

If the response to the first two questions is yes, and to the third no, then the project is unrelated to an increase in population. It is more likely, however, that the size of projects, such as schools, are based on projected growth in population. In this situation, the incremental (rather than average) cost should be allocated to the new development, if the data are available.[17] It may be argued that since growth is already projected and thus a built-in factor, the approval of a specific development results in the addition of only part of the projected population. Thus, unless the population increment from new development does not exceed the projected level, the decision to provide the facility is independent of the approval of a request for new development.

NET FISCAL EFFECT (See Chapter Six)

The revenue and expenditure estimates discussed in the preceding sections can be aggregated in a table similar to the model presented below, to obtain the net fiscal impact on a county of a proposed development.[18] It should be noted that the revenues and expenditures from the existing land use functions should be subtracted from the totals to obtain the net effect of the development.

---

17. In some instances, the incremental cost of increasing capital outlays is below average cost, as in the case of certain educational facilities; to build a high school for 2,000 students, other factors being equal, is less expensive, on a per student basis, then a high school designed to facilitate 800 students. However, the per unit cost of providing highways and certain utilities can increase as the number of units increases.

18. See Table 34, p. 83, for a corresponding table which summarizes the Albemarle County study.

County Revenue-Expenditure Summary

Development Type	Development-Linked Revenue to County	Development-Linked County Operating Expenditures	County Capital Expenditures	
			Development-Linked	Related to Entire County
Residential				
Non-Residential				
Subtotal				
Less: Existing Land Use				
Total	\$W	\$X	\$Y	\$Z
\$W - (\$X + \$Y + \$Z) = $\pm$ \$ Net Fiscal Effect				

A GENERAL GUIDE TO THE STUDY AND ITS APPLICATION

The remainder of this paper, consisting of six chapters and related appendices, presents a case study of a proposed development in Albemarle County, Virginia. Each chapter discusses a step in the analysis of the fiscal impact on Albemarle County of the development, and in an appendix, the fiscal effect the development will have on the State of Virginia is estimated.

The case study can be used by planners and developers as a prototype for evaluating the net fiscal effect of a proposed project. Further, because the method of analysis presented allows for the identification of particular revenues and expenditures associated with various kinds of development (i.e., single family, apartment, commercial, etc.), the results of such a study can suggest policy alternatives for offsetting negative fiscal effects, should they be predicted.

Finally, the case study can be used by members of zoning boards, lawyers, and other interested parties as a guide for evaluating fiscal impact statements submitted on proposed development projects.

CHAPTER ONE
BACKGROUND OF ALBEMARLE COUNTY

Albemarle County, Virginia (population: 40,000), which surrounds the city of Charlottesville (population: 39,000), is one of the smaller metropolitan areas of the State. Virginia has followed the nation in the pattern of population growth in the past decade, with rural areas losing population, cities, including Charlottesville, showing only minor increases, and over 60 percent of the growth occurring in the suburbs of its cities.

The specific area in Albemarle County to be examined is Phase I of the Hollymead Development (See Figure 1), which is the first part of the proposed "North Rivanna Community Cluster." The total Cluster area consists of 3,510 acres and is envisioned to contain between 18,000 and 23,000 residents--equal to about half the present County population. Hollymead Phase I is representative of the total development; the value of residential property as a share of the total and the mix of housing types does not deviate significantly between Hollymead Phase I and the total Cluster.

It should be noted that in 1963, the City of Charlottesville annexed a portion of Albemarle County. Population data used in the section of this study, which discusses the County's general demographic and socioeconomic characteristics, have been adjusted to reflect the annexation; however, adjusted data on socioeconomic characteristics are not readily available. In a subsequent section which examines specific revenue and expenditure trends for the County, the 1963 annexation is taken into account.

Figure 1

ALBEMARLE COUNTY, VIRGINIA

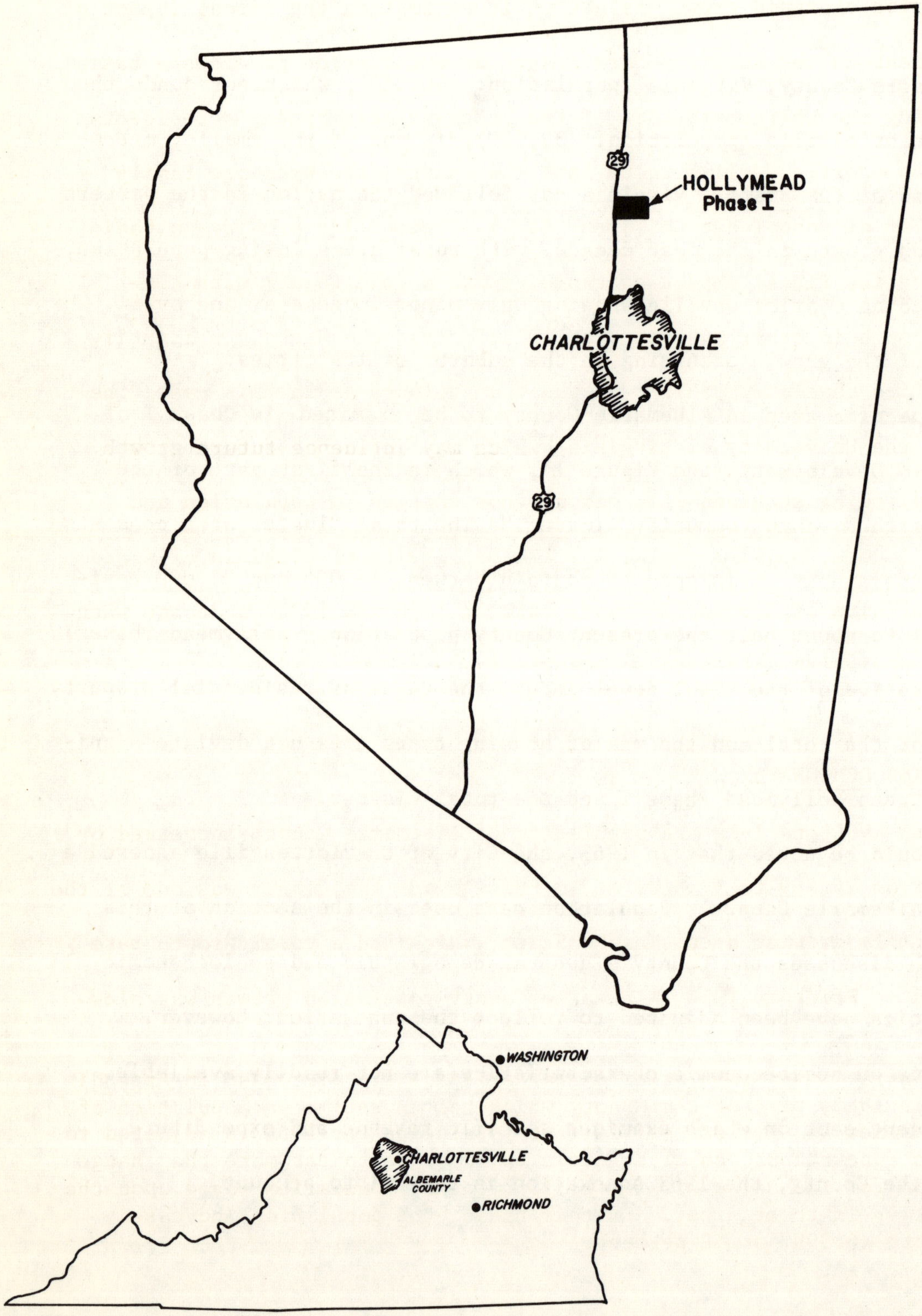

DEMOGRAPHIC AND SOCIOECONOMIC CHARACTERISTICS

There are two major reasons why close examination of the changes in the demographic and socioeconomic characteristics of Albemarle County during a period of rapid growth is useful in estimating the fiscal impact of new development in the County. First, such an examination provides a basis for predicting the characteristics of the proposed development's residents (e.g., what proportion will migrate into the County, the expected family income, number of school-age children, etc.). Second, it provides a basis for comparing the fiscal impact of rapid growth in the County with the effect of growth in other suburban jurisdictions in the State, to identify characteristics that are peculiar to the County (such as in this case, the location of the University of Virginia) which may influence future growth.

The following sections will discuss how changes in population and demography, income, housing costs, and the University of Virginia affected the fiscal affairs of Albemarle County between 1960 and 1970--a decade when the County population increased substantially.[19]

POPULATION AND DEMOGRAPHY

Between 1960 and 1970 the population of Albemarle County increased by 43 percent from 26,469 to 37,880.[20] In this decade the County was one of the six most rapidly growing areas in the State, which had a total growth rate of 17 percent. Prior to 1960, Albemarle County population growth was slow.

---

19. Intra-County population characteristics are discussed in Appendix A.

20. In 1963, part of the County which had an estimated population of 3,600 was annexed by Charlottesville; the population for 1960 is adjusted to reflect this annexation. An alternative approach is to estimate the change in population for the areas within the 1960 County boundaries based upon the 1970 population in those areas. On this basis, the population increased from 30,969 to 46,999, or 52 percent.

Two-thirds of the 1950-60 population growth was due to natural increase (births over deaths), and the balance as a result of net migration. However, between 1960 and 1965, 71 percent of the increase in population was due to migration.[21] An additional indication of recent growth is that 30 percent of all housing units in the County were built between 1965 and 1970.

The mobility of the population is reflected in the fact that of 34,877 residents five years of age and older, only 44 percent resided in the same house in 1970 as five years earlier. Of that balance, 5,795 moved within the County, 5,671 moved to the County from other parts of Virginia, and 5,067 (including 761 students) migrated from outside the State.[22]

In 1970 the fertility rate in the County, which is 3.13 children per woman ever married, is higher than the State average of 2.97 and the 2.90 average in six suburban Virginia counties.

Because of the County's large student population who attend the University of Virginia in Charlottesville, demographic patterns do not follow the State average. For example, 27.0 percent of the male population is between the ages of 15 and 24, compared to 17.8 percent in six suburban Virginia counties and 19.7 in the State. Only 38.1 percent of those between 18 and 24 years of age are in the labor force, less than half the rate for the State.

---

21. State of Virginia, Division of Planning, "Projections and Economic Base Analysis of the Charlottesville Metropolitan Area," October 1967.

22. This and other demographic data are from the U.S. Bureau of the Census, 1970 Census of Population, General Housing Characteristics and Number of Inhabitants--Virginia, HC(1)-A48 (Washington, D.C.: U.S. Government Printing Office, 1972).

INCOME

Between 1959 and 1969, the median family income in the County increased 98 percent, from $4,516 to $8,949. This growth in income was somewhat above the State average growth rate (82 percent); however, the State median income ($9,049) continues to be slightly above the County median. An examination of seven suburban Virginia counties indicates the same rate of income growth as Albemarle County, or 98 percent, in the 1959-1969 time period.

As of 1969, 20 percent of Albemarle County families had an income over $15,000--a measure of affluent households--which is the same proportion as the State average. However, 1.2 percent of all families earned incomes over $50,000--more than twice the State average for this income group. At the other end of the income spectrum, 13.0 percent of the County population was below the poverty level compared to the State average of 12.3 percent.[23] Mean income in the County (not available for 1959) was $11,103 in 1969, or about 5.0 percent above the State average.[24] These statistics do not reflect the impact of the 1963 annexation, in which the County lost a number of residents with income above the County mean; had part of the County not been annexed, it is likely that family income levels would have increased at a slightly faster rate.

---

23. Poverty level is defined by the Census Bureau on the basis of criteria such as size of household. The poverty threshold in 1969 ranged from $1,487, for unrelated individuals over 65, to $6,116, for non-farm families with six or more residents. For a detailed definition see U.S. Bureau of the Census, 1970 Census of Population, General Social and Economic Characteristics, PC(1)-C48 (Washington, D.C.: U.S. Government Printing Office, 1972) Appendix B.

24. The difference between median and mean income in the County and the State is due in part to the comparatively high proportion of families earning over $50,000. In addition, the farm population of the County, which comprises 5.8 percent of the County total, had a mean income in 1969 of $12,544, compared to $7,920 for all farm families in the State.

The relatively low County median income structure is due to the comparatively low wage scale. For most occupations, median earnings are below the State level; as examples, in 1969 the median salary for professional and managerial workers who were County residents was $10,735, and in the State, $11,236. For craftsmen and foremen, the median salary in 1969 was $6,033 in the County and $7,165 in the State.

Manufacturing is the major source of employment in the County, absorbing 56 percent of the private sector labor force. Although manufacturing employment rose sharply between 1967 and 1970 (from 3,305 to 4,114 employees), increasing more rapidly than the rate of population growth, the average wage per manufacturing employee (not necessarily a County resident) in April 1970 remained below the State level.[25] Agriculture continues to be an important element in the County economy; in 1969 the market value of farm products was $7.9 million, or 1.4 percent of the State total.[26]

COST OF HOUSING

The median value of owner-occupied housing in the County increased 100 percent between 1960 and 1970, from $11,100 to $22,200; median gross rent payments increased 180 percent from $54 to $151.[27] By comparison, the median value of owner-occupied housing in the State increased 59 percent,

---

25. U.S. Bureau of the Census, 1970 County Business Patterns: U.S. Summary, CBP-70-1, (Washington, D.C.: U.S. Government Printing Office, 1971). Employment is concentrated in three manufacturing enterprises, which in 1971 employed 3,050 workers.

26. U.S. Bureau of the Census, 1969 Census of Agriculture--Virginia, Section 2 (Washington, D.C.: U.S. Government Printing Office, 1972).

27. Gross rent is defined as contract rent plus cost of utilities and fuels if these items are paid by the renter in addition to rent. The median contract rent in the County during 1970 was $121/month.

from $10,800 to $17,200, while median gross rent rose 62 percent, from $71 to $115 per month.[28]

As a result of the comparatively high cost of housing in 1970, the ratio of house value to income for the County was 2.5 while the State ratio was 1.9.[29] Median gross annual rent constituted 20.2 percent of median income in the County compared to 15.3 percent in the State. It should be noted that these relationships do not represent median house values relative to income of those residing in single unit dwellings, since their income is generally above the level of multi-unit residents. However, since the proportion of owners to renters is the same in the County as in the State (more than two to one), the relative comparison is meaningful. There is little question that the price of both owner and renter occupied housing in the County is above the State level, although median income is somewhat below the State average.

IMPACT OF THE UNIVERSITY OF VIRGINIA

According to the 1970 Census of Population, 4,164 (or 11 percent) of the County residents are college students, compared to 2.9 percent in the State. Since of these, only 213 students attend other State supported institutions and 298 attend private colleges, it can be assumed that the

28. The impact of annexation in 1963 is not estimated. Median gross rents are the highest for any county in the State with the exception of Fairfax. U.S. Bureau of the Census, 1960 Census of Housing, States and Small Areas--Texas-Wyoming, Vol. I, Part 8, Table 48-97 (Washington, D.C.: U.S. Government Printing Office, 1963); and 1970 Census of Housing, Detailed Housing Characteristics--Virginia, HC(1)-B, Tables 61 and 62 (Washington, D.C.: U.S. Government Printing Office, 1972).

29. One factor explaining the high County cost of housing is the high proportion of new units. In suburban areas of Virginia, newer housing units have higher average value compared to older units.

majority attend the University of Virginia.[30] However, University of Virginia estimates differ sharply. According to a recent University study[31] it is estimated that only 1,454 of the University's students considered Albemarle County their place of residence in 1970-71. Based on Census data and the fact that 1971-72 enrollment at the University of Virginia increased by 14 percent since 1970, it is estimated that between 3,300 and 3,800 students whose permanent residence is not Albemarle County are currently living there.

Since the vast majority of students rent rather than own housing, a considerable share of rental units available in the County are probably occupied by students. With projected increases in University enrollments to about 15,000 by 1980 and the rising trend for students to live in the County, the impact of this segment of the population[32] has to be taken into account in estimates of the future housing costs, income, and the overall demographic structure of the County.[33]

---

30. There are no other colleges in or within commuting distance of the County.

31. University of Virginia, The University of Virginia in the Decade of the Seventies, Charlottesville, Va., April 1972.

32. An extent of the impact on the County of the number of college students can be estimated by comparing the proportion of expected males between the ages of 15-24 and the actual number in the County. Based on State averages, there are 1,425 more males and slightly more females in the County in this group than would be expected.

33. For additional data on college enrollment see Appendix B.

CHAPTER TWO
REVENUE AND EXPENDITURE TRENDS IN ALBEMARLE COUNTY

To estimate the fiscal impact of a large residential and non-residential development, it is useful to determine the patters of change in County revenues and expenditures during a recent period of rapid growth. For purposes of this portion of the study, an eight year period, beginning with fiscal 1964, will be used in order to avoid distortions in the data due to the 1963 annexation.

Since this study focuses only on the fiscal impact of Hollymead Phase I, comprehensive estimates of total County revenues and expenditures, based on 1964-1972, trends will not be made.[34]

LOCAL REVENUES

As shown in Table 1, local revenues increased by 281 percent between fiscal 1964 and 1972. This sharp rise was primarily due to the expansion of the property tax base, which increased from $34.2 million to $92.1 million.[35] In view of changes in the assessed to market value ratios, the 169 percent tax base increase only approximates market change in

---

34. A comprehensive analysis would require that revenues be projected (assuming no changes in the present tax structure and rates) while expenditures necessary to maintain a given level of public services would also be projected for a particular time period. An estimation would than be made of the difference between revenues and expenditures (the residual, or gap) including the impact of anticipated changes in population resulting from new development.

35. Adjusted to reflect tax collections as of June 30, 1972.

TABLE 1

1964-1972 Change in Albemarle County Revenue

Local Revenue Source	1964	1972	Change 1964-1972
Real and Personal Property Taxes	$1,410,735	$4,730,847	235%
Local Sales Tax	--	427,528	--
Utility Tax	--	810,408	--
Motor Vehicle License	101,402	194,782	92
Other Local Revenue*	212,079	413,106	95
TOTAL LOCAL REVENUE	$1,724,216	$6,576,671	281%

* Includes interest on bank deposits, clerk's fees, taxes for recordation of deeds, fines; $100,000 from City of Charlottesville for annexation in 1964 was excluded.

SOURCE: County of Albemarle Budget 1965-66, 1971-72; County Revenue Statement, June 30, 1972

property value. Property tax revenues increased more rapidly than the property tax base, from $1.4 million in 1964 to $4.7 million in 1972, or 235 percent. The difference between the two rates of increase, as presented in Table 2, is attributable to the rise in the effective tax rate from $0.53 per $100 market value to $0.79 per $100 market value.[36] A comparison of this property tax rate with other Virginia counties indicates that only five had effective tax rates greater than $1.00 in 1971.[37] Among seven

36. Between fiscal 1962 and 1970, the effective tax rate increase in Albemarle County was 69.6 percent. By comparison, the average effective tax rate for all Virginia jurisdictions during the same time period was 19.6 percent. J. L. Knapp, "Fiscal Prospects and Alternatives," Virginia Division of State Planning, April 1971.

37. Of these five counties, four have the largest population in the State. The fifth, Stafford County, had a population rate increase of 45.7 percent between 1960 and 1970.

TABLE 2

1964-1972 Change in Albemarle County Assessed Property Value

Assessed Property Value[a]	1964	1972	Change 1964-1972
Real Estate	$17,305,040	$52,191,130	201%
Personal Property	10,589,070[b]	19,307,690	82
Public Service Corporation	6,346,863	11,543,063	80
TOTAL ASSESSED PROPERTY	$34,240,973	$83,041,883	143%
Effective Real Property Tax Rate	0.53	0.79	49%
Property Tax as Percent of Total Revenue	82.0%	71.9%	N.A.

a. Estimate for 1971-1972. Actual final tax receipts indicate property value subject to tax was about 11 percent above preliminary estimates.

b. For 1964 farm machinery and livestock are household effects included. These personal property taxes eliminated in 1965 and 1966.

SOURCE: County of Albemarle Budget, 1965-66, 1971-72; County Revenue Statement, June 30, 1972.

counties in the 30,000 to 40,000 population range only one--rapidly growing Loudoun County--had a tax rate higher than Albemarle County. Although there is a strong positive correlation between the population base (density), the rate of change in the density, and the change in property tax rates, it is not feasible to determine the cause for this relationship without further analyses.[38] However, it is apparent that the tax rise in Albemarle County is typical of rapidly growing counties within Virginia.

38. The correlation coefficient between the tax rate (dependent variable) and population density per square mile and the rate of population growth (independent variables) is r = .72 for all Virginia counties between 1960 and 1970.

Real property taxes as a share of all property taxes increased from 50.5 percent in 1964 to 62.9 percent in 1972, since the share of personal property taxes decreased. This is attributable to the slow rise in the value of automobiles (which in Virginia are subject to personal property tax) compared to real property. However, because two additional local tax sources were introduced in the 1960's (utility and sales taxes), the dependence on the property tax as a local revenue source was reduced. Without these new revenue sources the property tax rate would have had to increase at a steeper rate in order to maintain the same level of public services.

As a result of increasing property tax rates and the utilization of new revenue sources, the County's bonded debt has actually decreased in recent years, since most capital outlays were funded from current revenues. This is atypical of growing suburban communities in the nation.

LOCAL OPERATING EXPENDITURES

Data in Table 3 indicate that public education dominated local operating expenditures. The school operating costs (excluding debt service, which is considered by the County as an operating expenditure) comprised 76.7 percent of the fiscal 1964 budget, and 76.1 percent of the fiscal 1972 budget. One factor explaining the high local education costs in the County is the relatively low level of State payment as a share of the total cost. State grants in 1970-1971 were 25.9 percent of all school operating revenues received by the County Department of Education, compared to an average of 31.6 percent for all Virginia counties.[39]

---

39. Superintendent of Public Instruction, Annual Report, Virginia State Board of Education, December 1971, Table 45. This difference is due to the State allocation formula, which is based, in part, on property value. The County per student value is considered above the State average, thus, the County is not eligible for supplemental grants.

TABLE 3

Albemarle County-Funded Operating Expenditures

Function[a]	June 30, 1964	June 30, 1972	Change 1964-1972
School Operating	$1,161,526	$3,379,667	191%
School Debt Service	145,805	502,529	245
General Government[b]	159,544	532,372	228
Law Enforcement (Police)	31,511	80,419	155
Prison Care	15,945	24,221	52
Fire Prevention	26,621	102,766	286
Library	32,465	107,440	231
Health (Including Mental Health and Lunacy Commission)	41,205	106,453	158
Agriculture and Home Economics	14,754	31,439	113
Landfill	31,027	57,982	87
Recreation	---	11,315	--
Utility Services[c] (Earlysville Dam)	--	13,377	--
TOTAL	$1,660,403	$4,940,980	198%
County Population	29,800	40,000	34.2%
Per Capita Expenditure (Excluding Education)	$11.84	$26.47	124%

a. This list excludes welfare costs, both for 1964 and 1972. Welfare costs for 1972 are estimated at $61,212. Several minor functions, which result in a cumulative total of less than two percent of all expenditures are also excluded. School debt service is listed by the County as an operating expenditure.

b. Including Department of Finance, Board of Supervisors, County Executive, Engineering Department, Board of Equalization and Elections, Recorder of Documents, County Share of Planning District, Social Security and other County employee benefits, courts and miscellaneous expenditures.

c. Water and sewer services are funded from user charges, and are not part of the County budget.

SOURCE: County of Albemarle Budget, 1965-1966 and 1971-1972.

Special attention should be paid to three additional factors affecting increased County expenditures between 1964 and 1972: growth in population; higher wages in the public sector; and changes in the level or quality of services.

Increase in Total and Student Population. It is estimated that the population of the County increased by about 10,200 persons in the eight year period between 1964 and 1972, or 34.2 percent. However, the number of students in public schools increased faster than the rate of population growth. In the same eight year period, average daily attendance (ADA) increased from 5,516 to 7,914, or 43.4 percent increase.[40] Local operating cost and debt service increased from $309 to $491 per student.

Wage Increases. Wages for public employees have risen sharply between 1964 and 1972 in all parts of the nation. In Albemarle County, the majority of County employees are teachers and other personnel employed by the school system. The average annual salary for elementary school teachers increased from $4,887 to $7,677 between fiscal 1964 and 1972, an increase of 57.1 percent. Annual salaries for high school teachers increased from $5,213 to $8,898, or 70.2 percent. Salaries for other instructional employees increased proportionately. If increases in education salaries are parallel to increases for other public employees in the County, the major factor in the increase in per-unit cost is due to higher unit salaries. As examples of other increases, the sheriff's salary increased 66 percent, and the jailer's 84 percent between 1964 and 1972.

Changes in Level and Quality of Services. Not all changes in expenditures can be fully explained by wage increase or population growth.

---

40. More than 80 percent of the increase in enrollment occurred between 1964 and 1969.

In education, between fiscal 1964 and 1972, total operating costs per ADA increased from $340 to $791, an increase of 133 percent. This is about twice the rate of increase in teachers' salaries.

Since teacher-student ratios were only reduced slightly between 1964 and 1972 (one teacher per 17.8 ADA in 1964 and one teacher per 17.2 ADA in 1972), non-instructional salary expenditures presumably increased at a faster rate than expenditures for teachers.[41]

A more detailed study of County functions would be required to determine what unit costs have increased or decreased as a result of economies or diseconomies of scale and changes in the quality of services, however examples of changes in service provision can be noted. The number of paid fire department employees increased sharply, from 2 to 46 in the eight year interval. In 1964, only $820 was allocated directly for salaries and $17,600 to volunteer fire departments, while in 1972, $52,190 was appropriated for firemen's salaries, and $48,071 for volunteer fire departments. In addition, as the population of the County increased, a number of support services were greatly expanded; the growth of the planning and engineering departments are examples of increasing demand for general government functions.

LOCAL CAPITAL EXPENDITURES

Capital expenditures paid from current revenues have been increasing since fiscal 1964 when these expenditures (excluding debt service) totaled only $34,152. In fiscal 1967, capital outlays (primarily for schools but but including airport improvements and watershed projects) totaled $2,556,235. In fiscal 1972, non-school projects were allocated $1,372,182.

---

41. This increase may, however, reflect an error in the State Department of Education data.

CHAPTER THREE
REVENUE ESTIMATES: HOLLYMEAD PHASE I

In this section of the study, revenues accruing to Albemarle County from the households and business enterprises to be located in the Hollymead Phase I section of the North Rivanna Community Cluster are estimated.[42] All revenue estimates are based on actual County receipts for fiscal 1972.

HOUSEHOLDS

The County estimates of the expected residential density of Hollymead Phase I are shown in Table 4. These estimates are consistent with other

TABLE 4

Residential Density for Dwellings in Hollymead Phase I

Dwelling Type	Density Per Unit	% of Total Units
Single Family	3.7	44%
Townhouse	3.2	31
Apartment	2.6	25
Weighted Mean	3.27	N.A.

SOURCE: Albemarle County Department of Planning, Staff Report: Hollymead, Revised February 1972 (mimeo).

42. Appendix C presents a revenue-expenditure analysis of the entire North Rivanna Community Cluster.

surveys and the weighted average of 3.27 is close to the 1970 average of 3.22 for all occupied units in the County.

Revenue and expenditure estimates assume <u>full occupancy</u> of housing units in the Hollymead Development, as well as full utilization of commercial space allocated for the development. On the basis of migration patterns between 1965 and 1970, it is assumed that about 35 percent of those moving to the new development will have previously resided in the County; as a result, a number of housing units in other parts of the County will be vacated. It will be further assumed that vacated housing units will be re-occupied by households with demographic and socioeconomic characteristics similar to the previous residents. (The same assumptions will be applied in the case of business enterprises which will locate in Hollymead Phase I.)

Depending on the demand for housing at various price levels, it may be that as a result of the shift in residence, certain substandard housing units may be abandoned. Business enterprises moving to the new shopping centers may also result in the closing of some existing enterprises. However, in the absence of evidence that substandard units have been abandoned during periods of growth in Charlottesville or the County, these possibilities will not be considered.

Since operating and capital expenditures between fiscal 1964 and 1972 have risen at a faster rate than revenues, there is likely to be a gap between revenues and expenditures if the historical trend continues. This analysis does not incorporate potential changes in the tax base or tax rates to eliminate this potential gap. Anticipated non-local revenue, particularly from federal revenue sharing, are exluded in these computations.

REAL PROPERTY TAXES

Because approximately 78 percent of total property value in Hollymead Phase I will be of a residential nature, it is anticipated that households will be the County's major revenue source. The real property tax per unit in Hollymead can be estimated by multiplying the market value of each housing unit by the effective tax rate, which was $0.79 per $100 of market value in 1971-1972.[43] (The total market value of housing units is estimated at $22.8 million.) Table 5 contains the estimated real property tax per unit.

TABLE 5

Annual Real Property Tax for Hollymead Phase I

Dwelling Type	No. Units	Price Range[a]	Real Property Tax Per Unit
Single Family	358	$27,000-$28,000 (25%) $35,000 (50%) $45,000-$48,000 (25%) Weighted Mean: $35,500	$280.45
Townhouse	256	$24,000-$27,000 Weighted Mean: $25,500	$201.45
Apartment[b]	199	$18,000	$142.20

a. Estimates made by developer.
b. Two and three bedroom apartments.

43. Albemarle County Department of Planning, Staff Report: Hollymead, Revised February 1972 (mimeo). The anticipated market value estimates were provided by the developer to the Department of Planning.

PERSONAL PROPERTY AND SALES TAXES

ESTIMATING HOUSEHOLD INCOME

To estimate personal property taxes and to determine sales tax receipts, it is necessary to approximate the likely income of Hollymead Phase I residents. An analysis of 16 census tracks from five suburban counties in Virginia (composed almost exclusively of single family dwellings, most which were built since 1965) indicates that house value to income ratios do not deviate significantly as income rises.[44]

TABLE 6

Ratio of House Value to Annual Household Income for Hollymead Phase I

Dwelling Type	Weighted Mean Price	Unit Value to Income Ratio	Estimated Annual Household Income
Single Family	$35,500	1.90	$18,637
Townhouse	$25,500	2.00	$12,750
Apartment	$18,000*	1.95	$ 9,231

* Apartment rents are based on a newspaper survey of newer units in 1971-1972, and range from $165 to $190. This rent payment results in a gross rent multiplier (unit value divided by yearly rent payments) of 8.5. This is considered a conservative multiplier in the County for new income-producing property.

Table 6 shows dwelling unit to income relationships estimated for the Hollymead development.

44. Data from U.S. Bureau of the Census, Census of Population and Housing, Census Tracts, PHC(1)226 and PHC(1)173, shows the following income to house value ratio in selected suburban census tracts in Virginia:

1969 Median Income	Ratio of 1970 Median House Value to 1969 Income
$10,000-$14,999	1.95
$15,000-$19,999	2.10
$20,000-$24,999	2.10
$25,000-$30,000	1.95

Since the median house value in Albemarle County was $22,200 in 1970, this would indicate that median house values are more than twice the level of median income ($8,949 in 1969).[45] This ratio is somewhat above national averages, but comparable to rapidly growing areas such as Fairfax County, Virginia. Nationally owner-occupied house values do not rise as fast as current income;[46] however, whether this relationship between house value and income holds for new housing as compared to all housing is questionable, particularly in an inflationary economy.[47] The mean income per housing unit for Hollymead residents will be $14,460 (in 1972 dollars). This compares to an estimated mean income for the County of $12,712 in fiscal 1972.

PERSONAL PROPERTY TAXES

Personal property taxes affecting households fall primarily on cars. However, boats and personal aircraft are also subject to this tax. The value of an automobile for tax purposes is determined by its National Automobile Dealers Association (NADA) loan value. The tax rate is $5.90 per $100 of the loan value.

The total value of personal property subject to the property tax is $1.2 million. Table 7 contains estimates of personal property tax by dwelling for Hollymead.

---

45. Average rent payments, which are $178 per month in apartment units, are 23 percent of income. This is above the metropolitan Virginia average of 20 percent. U.S. Bureau of Census, 1970 Census of Housing, Metropolitan Housing Characteristics, HC(2) (Washington, D.C.: U.S. Government Printing Office, 1972).

46. See, G. Katona, 1970 Survey of Consumer Finances (Ann Arbor, Michigan: University of Michigan Press, 1971), Table 3-13. These surveys do not distinguish between current and permanent income of owners and renters.

47. For a discussion of the demand for both owner-occupied and rental housing as a function of income, see F. deLeeuw, op. cit.

TABLE 7

Personal Property Tax Per Household in Hollymead Phase I

Dwelling Type	Average Car Loan Value[a]	Average Number of Cars Per Unit[a]	Other Taxable Personal Property[b]	Total Annual Personal Property Tax
Single Family	$1,100	1.5	$100	$103.25
Townhouse	950	1.4	80	83.19
Apartment	750	1.2	60	56.64

a. Estimate of number of cars and their average value is based on data associating cars with income as shown in U.S. Bureau of the Census, Consumer Buying Indicators, Series P-65, May 1972.

b. The number of boats and personal aircraft by income group in the County is not known. It is assumed that one out of every 25 households will own a boat, one out of every 500 households, a private plane.

STATE SALES TAX

One third of the sales tax collected by the State is redistributed to counties on the basis of the number of school age children,[48] independent of collections from the jurisdiction. To determine County revenues per student, the total 1972 receipts ($71,235) are divided by the estimated school age population, resulting in a per student payment of $83.76. It should be noted that this revenue appears as part of State aid to education in the County budget.

Table 8 shows the sales tax revenue by dwelling type.

LOCAL SALES TAX

Average County sales tax receipts (1.0 percent) in fiscal 1972 was $427,528 or $40.55 per occupied dwelling unit. Average household income in the County in fiscal 1972 is estimated at $12,712 (slightly above the State

48. On p. 49 of this paper estimates are made of the number of school age children per dwelling unit.

TABLE 8

Redistribution of State Sales Tax Revenue
Per Household in Hollymead Phase I

Dwelling Type	Number of Students	Annual Revenue Per Unit
Single Family	1.05	$87.94
Townhouse	0.90	75.38
Apartment	0.43	36.02

average). If all consumption were to take place in the County, approximately 0.45 percent of gross household income would be taxed.[49] (This figure is for the average size household. Larger households, given the same income level, have higher consumption for goods such as food, which are subject to the State sales tax.)

The balance of personal income is not subject to the sales tax. This includes tax payments, savings, expenditures for housing and services, etc. As income increases, the proportion of income subject to the sales tax decreases. Utilizing the 0.45 percent ratio, approximately $57 in sales tax would be collected from the average County household, $62 from Hollymead households. On the basis of fiscal 1972 tax collection, up to 71 percent of the potential consumption actually takes place in the County, the balance primarily in Charlottesville.[50]

---

49. Based on expenditure patterns shown in U.S. Department of Labor, Bureau of Labor Statistics, <u>1971 Urban Family Budgets</u> (Washington, D.C.: U.S. Government Printing Office, April 1972).

50. The city of Charlottesville collected $1.3 million from the one percent local sales tax or $95.30 per household as shown in the <u>Charlottesville City Budget 1971-1972</u>. The average household income in the city is about the same as in Albemarle County. Actual purchase by County residents are likely to be somewhat below 71 percent, since part of the sales tax is derived from residents of surrounding counties and tourists.

Sales tax collections per household in the proposed development are estimated in Table 9.

TABLE 9

County Sales Tax Revenues
Per Household in Hollymead Phase I

Dwelling Type	Mean Income Per Unit	Sales Tax as Percent of Income	Expected Annual Sales Tax	Annual County Share (71 Percent)
Single Family	$18,637	0.41	$76.41	$54.25
Townhouse	12,750	0.45	57.38	40.74
Apartment	9,231	0.48	44.31	31.46

OTHER TAXES

UTILITY TAXES

Three utility taxes are imposed on households by Albemarle County: (1) electric power--20 percent of the first $20 per month, or $4 per month maximum; (2) gas--20 percent of the first $10 per month, or a maximum of $2 per month; and (3) telephone (on the base charge)--20 percent or about $1.40 per month.

In the absence of utility company records, it is difficult to estimate average payments per structure with any precision. Telephone taxes are relatively constant, but other taxes on utilities vary with the size of the structure and number of appliances. It is estimated that of the total

$816,408 in annual County revenues from utilities in 1971-1972, $126,100 was paid by business enterprises.[51] Thus, $609,308, or $58 per unit, is paid by households.

Table 10 presents estimates of utility taxes for the Hollymead development by dwelling type.[52]

TABLE 10

Utility Taxes Per Household in Hollymead Phase I

Dwelling Type	Annual G & E Tax	Annual Telephone Tax	Total Annual Utility Tax
Single Family	$60.00	$16.80	$76.80
Townhouse	48.00	16.80	64.80
Apartment	33.60	16.80	50.40

ABC STATE TAX

Alcoholic Beverage Control (ABC) taxes are distributed to County on a per capita basis. In fiscal 1972, the County received $132,797 from the State of Virginia, based upon <u>1960</u> Census of Population residence statistics.[53] State payments in fiscal 1972 averaged $3.50 per capita.

---

51. Commercial and industrial enterprises are taxed at the rate of 10 percent on the first $300 in utility bills per month, and at 2 percent on bills in excess of $300. To estimate the amount paid by industry and commerce, the 474 business enterprises were grouped by the number of employees: it was assumed that enterprises with three or less employees paid $150 in taxes annually; those having 4-499 employees, $400; and the three facilities with over 500 employees, $4,000 in utility taxes.

52. These values are above the County Planning Department estimate of $48 in utility taxes for each unit in the North Rivanna Community Cluster.

53. It is assumed that in 1972, 1970 Census of Population statistics will be utilized.

Table 11 shows the estimates of ABC tax distribution by dwelling type.

TABLE 11

Distribution of ABC Tax Revenue
Per Household in Hollymead Phase I

Dwelling Type	Density Per Unit	Annual Revenue Per Unit
Single Family	3.7	$12.95
Townhouse	3.2	11.20
Apartment	2.6	9.10

HOUSEHOLD REVENUE SUMMARY

Total County revenues anticipated from the residential portion of Hollymead Phase I are shown in Table 12.[54]

BUSINESS ENTERPRISES

The developer of the North Rivanna Community Cluster plans to allocate 30.6[55] acres of land contained in Sub-Section C and E of Hollymead Phase I

54. The local tax structure is slightly regressive, which is typical of most local government. Thus, a household earning $9,200 pays about 3.3 percent of its income in local taxes, while a household earning twice this level pays about 2.9 percent of its income locally. This is not due to the real property tax, which is likely to be proportional for new suburban housing within the income range specified--rather, it is due to other local revenue sources, such as the utility and sales taxes.

55. At present, about 960 retail workers generate $690,000 in County sales taxes, or $720 per employee. Using data from Table 9, it is estimated that about $36,000 is anticipated in additional sales taxes accruing to the County from residents of Hollymead; this amount would accommodate an additional 50 retail employees. Based on the experience of Fairfax County, this would suggest a net increase of two acres of commercial space rather than 30.6 acres as estimated by the developer. The balance of commercial space allocated for retail business (28.6 acres) would have to attract consumers from other retail establishments in the County, the City of Charlottesville, and

(cont'd p.42)

TABLE 12

Total Annual County Revenues From Households in Hollymead Phase I

Revenue Source	Single Family	Townhouse	Apartment	Revenue as a Percent of Total: Single Family	Townhouse	Apartment
Real Property Tax	$280.45	$201.45	$142.20	43.6%	40.2%	41.0%
Personal Property Tax	103.25	83.19	56.64	16.1	16.6	16.3
Local Sales Tax (1%)	54.25	40.74	31.46	8.4	8.1	9.1
State Sales Tax. Redist.	87.94	75.38	36.02	13.6	15.0	10.4
Utilities Tax	76.80	64.80	50.40	11.9	12.9	14.5
Motor Vehicle Registration	15.00	14.00	12.00	2.3	2.8	3.5
ABC Redistribution	12.95	11.20	9.10	2.1	2.2	2.6
Other Revenues[a]	12.60	10.80	8.80	2.0	2.2	2.6
TOTAL PER UNIT[b]	$643.24	$501.56	$346.62	100.0%	100.0%	100.0%
No. Units	358	256	199	358	256	199
TOTAL REVENUE	$230,279.	$130,703.	$68,977.	53.5%	30.4%	16.1%

a. Includes fees, fines, etc., and are estimated at $3.40 per capita.
b. Excluding State sales tax redistribution.

for business enterprises. This area will include commercial buildings, particularly shopping centers. The market value for real property in the commercial development is estimated at $6.5 million or 22 percent of the total market value for real property in Hollymead Phase I. It will be assumed that the commercial development will be completed concurrently with the residential development, avoiding a revenue lag for the County.

Using the 30.6 acre figure provided by the developer, it is estimated $78,792 in revenues will accrue to the County directly from commercial enterprises, as presented in Table 13.

TABLE 13

Annual County Revenues From Commercial[a] Development in Hollymead Phase I

Revenue Source	Annual Revenue
Real Property Tax Per Acre	$1,668
Personal Property Tax Per Acre	671
Utility Tax Per Acre	138
Total Tax Per Acre	2,477
Total Tax Revenues	75,792[b]
Estimated fees, licenses	3,000
TOTAL REVENUE FROM COMMERCIAL DEVELOPMENT	$78,792

a. Revenue calculations are based on comparative data on commercial development similar to the proposed development on a per acre basis.

b. There are 30.6 gross acres (24.9 net acres--gross acres less streets) for commercial development.

contiguous counties. The proportion of sales from each of these areas cannot be estimated without additional data on the characteristics of the anticipated retail establishment. However, the only net sales tax gain to the County (in addition to those provided by Hollymead residents) would be sales "captured" from other jurisdictions which would otherwise not accrue to the County.

REAL PROPERTY TAXES FROM EXISTING LAND USE

Hollymead Phase I contains 227.7 acres of land which was previously zoned agricultural; the average assessed value of this land was $249 per acre or $56,772.[56] Thus, the taxes collected by the County prior to subdivision would be $5.90 per $100 of assessed value, or $3,349 per annum. These revenues are not offset by any County expenditure, since the land is undeveloped. (This estimate of County revenue from existing land use will be used in calculating the net revenue-expenditure difference in Chapter Six.)

FEDERAL REVENUE SHARING

Federal revenue sharing, which is tentatively estimated at approximately $10 per capita for Albemarle County, is excluded from this analysis for several reasons. According to the provisions of the revenue sharing legislation,[57] there are three factors which affect the amount a jurisdiction receives: population, income, and tax effort. The population base used for the purposes of the calculations is the Census of Population, which is taken once each decade. Although the legislation permits the use of estimated values, it does not appear feasible to determine annual changes in population and income for each jurisdiction.

Further, since population is only one of three factors, unless low-income families migrate to Albemarle County or the tax effort is increased compared with other communities in the State, the increment in revenues would be small

---

56. Per acre values were computed from County assessment records provided by the Albemarle County Department of Finance.

57. The Revenue Sharing Act of 1972, P.L. 92-512.

even if annual population growth could be incorporated into the revenue sharing formula. Finally, since the current legislation expires in 1976 and there is some question as to its continuation beyond this date, the net fiscal effect of revenue sharing should not, at this time, be included in an analysis of the long-term fiscal effect of development.

CHAPTER FOUR
OPERATING EXPENDITURE ESTIMATES: HOLLYMEAD PHASE I

In this section of the study, County expenditures for public services will be allocated among households and commercial-industrial enterprises. Expenditures are allocated for each type of unit in the Hollymead development on the basis of likely demand for public services.

Public services can be grouped into two categories: (1) those utilized primarily by households; and (2) those utilized by both households and business enterprises. While it can be argued that business benefits in the long run from all public services, or that costs allocated to commercial and industrial enterprises are shifted forward to the consumer, these viewpoints do not appear directly relevant to an analysis which focuses on the local fiscal impact of land use changes.

GENERAL METHODOLOGY

In order to estimate total operating expenditures incurred by the Hollymead Development and to allocate these expenditures between new households and business enterprises, it is necessary to begin with a summary of current operating expenditures in the County. The total County operating expenditures will be allocated between existing County households and business enterprises using their respective share of the real property base as a proxy for measuring public service use. In Albemarle County, this technique yields an allocation of 88.3 percent to County households and 11.7 percent to business enterprises. (In computing these percentages, 95 percent of farm property is counted as residential and 5 percent as business.)

It is recognized that property value is not the only determinant of public service use. In the case of households, income is a variable which should be adjusted for in allocating operating expenditures. To do this, total expenditures per capita or per dwelling unit should be obtained by dividing total County expenditures allocated to households by the number of residents or housing units in the County. These unit costs can then be adjusted for income.

For business enterprises, the use of criteria such as the number of employees per business has been suggested as an alternative means for measuring the utilization of public services.[58] However, this criterion cannot be applied in estimating operating expenditures for the Hollymead Development, since the developer has not provided data on the anticipated number of employees or the types of business planned for the development. In view of this limitation, it will be assumed that operating expenditures for business enterprises vary directly with the real property value of the businesses, based on the County average value per acre of commercial land. Therefore, operating expenditures will be allocated to Hollymead business enterprises in proportion to their share of the total residential and non-residential real property base of the County. Although detailed

---

58. An alternative approach would be to estimate public safety costs on the basis of the number of workers employed by commercial and industrial enterprises. W. Isard and R. Coughlin, Municipal Costs and Revenues Resulting From Community Growth (Boston, Mass.: Federal Reserve Bank of Boston, 1972). The approach suggested by these authors would result in a higher proportion of public safety cost allocated to business enterprises in the county than results when calculations are based on the ratio of property values.

assessment data by land use are not available for the County, estimates based on partial data from the County Assessor are shown in Table 14. The estimated share of the total property base represented by commercial and industrial property is slightly below the share

TABLE 14

Real Property Base in Albemarle County by Land-Use Type--Fiscal 1972

Land-Use Type	Employment/ Dwelling Units--1970	Assessed Value[a] (In Millions)	Market Value (In Millions)	Percent of Total Property Base
Industrial	4,114	$ 2.6	$19.4	4.5%
Commercial	3,274[b]	3.7	27.6	6.4
Acreage & Farms	--	10.8	80.6	18.7
Residential--Including Mobile Homes	11,693	40.3	304.3	70.4
TOTAL		$57.9	$431.9	100.0%

a. Total assessed value based on final fiscal 1972 property tax collections. Industrial assessed property estimates provided by County. Agricultural property market values based on data in U.S. Bureau of Census, _1969 Census of Agricultural--Virginia_ (Washington, D.C.: U.S. Government Printing Office, 1970), Pt. 24, Sec. 2, which indicates total 1969 values have not been increased in view of the lag between assessment of property and rise in land value. The value of commercial property is based on comparisons with other jurisdictions and the employment level.

b. All private sector employment except manufacturing in first quarter of 1970.

in four suburban Virginia counties.[59] Albemarle County, however, has a considerably larger share of agricultural property than most suburban Virginia counties, and twice the State average.

County-provided services used by both households and business enterprises include general government, law enforcement (police protection), fire prevention, and landfill. The allocation of operating expenditures for public services (by function) to household and business enterprises, based on estimated share of the real property base, is contained in Table 15.

TABLE 15

Allocation of Operating Expenditures for Services Used by Business Enterprises and Households in Albemarle County*

Function	Business	Households	TOTAL
General Government	$62,287	$470,085	$532,372
Law Enforcement (Police)	9,409	71,010	80,419
Fire Prevention	12,024	90,742	102,766
Landfill	6,784	51,198	57,982

*Consists of 6.4 percent commercial, 4.5 percent industrial, 0.8 percent farm (as business property). Prior to Hollymead Phase I, the inclusion of this development would increase the industrial and commercial share to 11.6% of the total.

59. Total industrial and commercial property in Albemarle County is estimated at 10.9 percent, somewhat below the average in four suburban Virginia counties--Henrico, Chesterfield, Fairfax and Prince William. U.S. Bureau of the Census, 1967 Census of Government-Taxable Property Value (Washington, D.C.: U.S. Government Printing Office, October 1968), Table 19.

ALLOCATION OF OPERATING EXPENDITURES FOR SERVICES USED BY HOUSEHOLDS

EDUCATION

Since approximately 69 percent of all County operating expenditures are made for public education, the estimation of the number of students from the Hollymead Development and the cost per student are sensitive parameters in determining incremental costs resulting from development.

NUMBER OF STUDENTS PER DWELLING UNIT

On the basis of examining similar housing units in Albemarle County, the County Planning Office estimates that in 1972-1973 Hollymead Phase I will send 683 students to public schools (377 elementary, 153 intermediate, 153 high school). These public school students will come from families residing in 614 units (single family and townhouse), with an average of 1.11 students per unit. However, an examination of the County report shows that all sub-sections of the Hollymead Development, with one exception, have a dwelling unit to student ratio of 0.98. It will therefore be assumed that the average anticipated density for non-apartment units in the Hollymead Development is 0.98, the value projected by the County staff.

The County's value (0.98) appears slightly low based on other estimates for single family units. For example, in its analysis of the Middle Run area, Fairfax County assumes 1.3 students per single family unit, and 1.1 student per townhouse.[60] The average number of public school students residing in single family units within Fairfax County is 1.13, while in

60. W. S. Lips, "Public Sector Cost-Revenue Analyses," Fairfax County Division of Planning, March 1971.

Prince Georges County, Maryland, it is 1.04.[61] However, the number of students per housing unit, as shown by an examination of a number of housing developments, indicates that the average number of students declines somewhat as a function of house age.[62] Thus, the average number of school-age children in an established community is likely to be lower than the number found in new developments.

In addition, the Albemarle County report notes that the number of residents in townhouses (3.2 per unit) is lower than the number in single family dwellings (3.6 per unit). Therefore, an estimate of 1.05 students per single family residence and 0.90 per townhouse will be utilized. The approach used to obtain this value is essentially to adopt the County estimate, but to allocate the 0.98 average between single family structures and townhouses.

Based on its survey, the County estimates 0.43 students per apartment unit. Since the developer stated that all apartments will be two and three bedroom units, this may be conservative. (A study of Fairfax County shows that families who reside in three bedroom apartments have as many students as single family homes.[63])

It has also been shown that as the share of apartments, as a proportion of total units in a County, increases, so does the number of students from apartments. This may be attributable to the rapid rise in the cost of single family homes; moderate income families with school aged children may not be able to afford such homes, and thus may remain in apartments for a longer time period. For purposes of this analysis, however, the 0.43 value for apartments provided by the County will be used.

---

61. T. Muller, Fiscal and Land Use Analysis of Prince Georges County, Volume II (Washington, D.C.: Doxiadis Urban Systems, Inc., June 1970).

62. Ibid, p. 93.

63. Fairfax County Planning Division, "Student Contribution From Apartments," 1966. See also, G. Sternlieb, The Garden Apartment Development (New Brunswick, N.J.: Rutgers University Press, 1964).

An alternative approach for estimating number of school children anticipated in a development, which is based on current fertility rates, is presented in Appendix D.

TABLE 16

Determination of Operating Expenditures Per Student (ADM) for Education in Albemarle County

Non-Local School Operating Revenues[a]	
State[b]	$2,556,548
Federal	368,693
Other Revenues	46,724
Non-Local Operating Revenues	2,971,965
Local School Operating Expenditures	
Total School Operating Cost[c]	6,351,631
Less Non-Local Revenue	2,971,965
Local Operating Expenditures	3,379,666
Sales Tax Redistribution[d]	712,355
TOTAL LOCAL OPERATING EXPENDITURES	$4,004,111
Local Operating Expenditures Per ADM (8.411 students)	$476.06

a. From Budget Report County of Albemarle, receipts as of June 30, 1972, p. 2. Average Daily Membership (ADM) values were provided by Albemarle County Department of Education.

b. Including sales tax redistribution.

c. Less debt service. School bus purchase not amortized.

d. State sales tax redistribution, as it is considered revenue from new households, is added to determine per pupil expenditures from new development.

EDUCATION COST PER STUDENT IN ALBEMARLE COUNTY

Table 16 shows how operating expenditures for education are determined for Albemarle County on a per student basis (ADM).[64]

EDUCATION COST PER STUDENT IN HOLLYMEAD PHASE I

In Table 17, County education operating expenditures per student for Hollymead Phase I are estimated. Included in this estimate are additional costs of $87,910 for adult education and other educational programs, which are allocated on the basis of $2.20 per capita. The estimated total number of students, on the basis of ratios shown in Table 17, is 692, or a weighted mean of 0.85 students for each of the 813 dwelling units proposed for Hollymead Phase I.

TABLE 17

Operating Expenditures Per Student for Education in Hollymead Phase I

Dwelling Type	Number Students Per Unit	Cost Per Unit (ADM)	Additional Education Costs	TOTAL
Single Family	1.05	$499.86	$8.14	$508.00
Townhouse	0.90	428.45	9.04	435.49
Apartment	0.43	204.71	5.72	210.43
Weighted Mean	0.85	$404.20	$6.93	$411.13

64. Average Daily Membership (ADM) is used instead of Average Daily Attendance (ADA) in these estimates because County estimates are in terms of ADM. There is a slight difference in value between these: ADM = 8,411; and ADA = 7,914.

INCLUSION OF STATE SALES TAX REDISTRIBUTION

An alternative means of computing education cost excludes the State sales tax redistribution as a household revenue item, and includes this State payment in determining cost per pupil. Table 18 shows the difference between including and excluding this tax for County per student education costs.

TABLE 18

The Impact of the State Sales Tax Redistribution

Dwelling Type	Revenue (Sales Tax Redistribution)	Per Student ADM Cost Excluding State Tax Aid	Per Student ADM Cost Including State Tax Aid	Differences in Per Student Cost
Single Family	$87.94	$499.86	$421.98	$77.88
Townhouse	75.38	428.45	361.70	66.75
Apartment	36.02	204.71	172.81	31.90

NON-EDUCATION OPERATING EXPENDITURES

The allocation to households of operating expenditures other than those for public education is a complex task. Although it is generally recognized that the demand for service is a function of many socioeconomic and demographic characteristics, the usual procedure is to allocate costs on a per capita basis. This approach assumes that the incremental cost of public services generated by new population is equal to the average cost of providing those services to the existing population. That is, it assumes no economies or diseconomies of scale associated with providing services to households in a developing area.

It is evident that a number of public services are related both to population and income. For example, certain social services, such as free health care and welfare, require the recipient to have an income below a certain minimum. The demand for other services, such as recreation, higher education and public libraries are likely to increase as income rises. Alternatively, household density is strongly related to demand for some services. For example, a household with three school-age children will utilize recreation facilities and libraries more than a household with no children. Finally, certain services, such as fire protection and recreation, are related to the distance from an existing fire station or playground. A detailed analysis of the most reliable techniques for allocating these costs is beyond the scope of this study.

Although some County service costs will be allocated on the basis of income and others on a per capita basis, it should be noted that the resulting deviation in costs is insignificant.[65] This may be a result of the fact that in Hollymead Phase I, households with the highest incomes (those living in single family homes) also have the highest density (3.7 persons per unit), while the households with lower incomes (those living in apartments) have lower densities (2.6 persons per unit).

---

65. Selected services (libraries, recreation, landfill) are allocated on the basis of income. It will be assumed that these services are income elastic; the coefficient of demand elasticity is assumed to be constant within the income range of households in the development. That is, for every dollar of income above the County average, demand (and the cost of providing the service) will increase by $0.50. For each dollar of income below the County average, demand (and cost of providing service to household) will decrease by $0.50. The elasticity coefficients are based, in part, on a study of 7,000 households in suburban Montgomery County, Maryland, with household incomes ranging from $5,600 to $22,000. The study shows the income elasticity of library use is 0.48, and recreation facilities 0.45. Fire and police service use was shown not to be related to income within the income range examined. See, Montgomery County Economic Development Commission, "The Relative Importance to Montgomery County of Selected Economic Activities," August 1970.

Since education and general government constituted 88 percent of all operating expenditures for Albemarle County in fiscal 1972, alternative assumptions regarding the method used to estimate the demand for (and to allocate the cost of) other services have little aggregate impact on total estimated expenditures.

A brief discussion of non-education expenditures and the basis on which they are allocated follows.

General Government. General government is the largest non-education County expenditure primarily because it covers a magnitude of services. Although it could be argued that higher income families have greater demand for certain services, such as planning and environment control, it is difficult to allocate most general government expenditures on any basis other than per capita.

Fire Prevention. Fire protection consists of limiting damage once fire has started, and providing services to prevent the occurrence of fires by education, inspection and related functions. Although the benefit of limiting damage to the household increases as the value of the property increases, the cost of providing the service may not. Three factors influence the cost of providing fire services: density; type of structure; and the likelihood of fire, which in residential areas is related to the age of the house and the socioeconomic characteristics of the residents.[66]

In the case of the Hollymead Development, the average density does not deviate sharply from other developed areas of the County, and the socioeconomic level of residents should be at or above the County average. However, since a fire sub-station is planned to service the entire North

66. T. Muller, op. cit., p. 48.

Rivanna Community Cluster, which will require new equipment, fire protection costs, at least initially, may be above the County average. In the absence of more detailed data, costs for this service will be allocated on a per capita basis.

Law Enforcement. Police protection costs appear to be highest in areas of high crime incidence, since the purpose of the service is preventative--to reduce crime. Although there is no reason to assume that the crime rate in the Hollymead Development will differ from that in the general population of the County, it can be argued that higher income residents may demand higher levels of police service. It has been shown that the cost for a given level of police protection appears to rise at a faster rate than increases in population.[67] However, an examination of the change in the number of State and local police required to serve the County as population increased indicates that the expansion of the force has been proportional to the increase in population.[68] Therefore, police protection will be allocated on a per capita basis.

Health and Welfare. The largest share of the County expenditure in the health and welfare category is for public health. Public health expenditures, administered by the joint City-County Department of Health, consist of: medical and dental care for indigents, and services provided for the general public. Services for the general public include nurses visiting public schools, immunization programs, and general health service. The County does not have a specific income criterion for "indigents," although

67. C. S. Shoup, Public Finance (Chicago, Ill.: Aldine Publishing Co., 1969), p. 116.

68. In 1964, there were 14 members of the local Albemarle County police force, and 10 State police. In 1972, the number increased to 19 local and 13 State police.

clinic facilities are to be utilized by only those who cannot afford private medical and dental care. Since the vast majority of Hollymead residents are not likely to be considered "indigent," one half of the County cost for public health will be allocated on a per capita basis to Hollymead residents for those services likely to be utilized by the general public. The balance of the services are not likely to be utilized by these new residents.[69] It is assumed that the number of welfare recipients in the County is not affected by the development.

Library Services. Library usage tends to increase with income, probably because of the correlation between income and education. Therefore, this service will be allocated on the basis of household income.

Utility Services. The demand for utilities, such as sewers, varies both with the size of household and with the size of land and improvements (which are linked to income). Therefore, this function will be allocated on the basis of household income.

Recreation. A number of studies have shown a correlation between income and the demand for recreation.[70] However, whether this is a valid assumption in an area where middle-income families may belong to private recreation clubs is uncertain. Despite this reservation, recreation will be allocated on the basis of household income.

Prison Care. This minor expenditure will be allocated on a per capita basis. However, if crime increases as a function of population density, prison care expenditure may rise more rapidly as population grows.

---

69. Based on conversations with Albemarle County Department of Health staff.

70. See, for example, M. Clawson, Land for the Future (Baltimore, Md.: John Hopkins University Press, 1960), pp. 124-230.

Agriculture and Home Economics. Part of this expenditure may serve agro-business interests in the County, rather than the total population. However, in view of the low expenditure level, it will be allocated on a per capita basis.

Summary of Non-Education Operating Expenditures. Tables 19 and 20 summarize the allocation of operating expenditures by type of housing unit. Table 19 shows non-education expenditures (library, landfill, recreation, and utilities) which are allocated on the basis of household income. Table 20 shows non-education expenditures (law enforcement, fire prevention, health and welfare, general government, prison care, and agriculture and home economics), which are allocated on a per capita basis.

TABLE 19

Allocation of Non-Education Operating Expenditures to Hollymead Phase I Households on the Basis of Household Income

Function	Mean Cost Per Unit	Single Family	Townhouse	Apartment
Library	$10.19	$12.53	$10.19	$8.76
Landfill	4.86	5.98	4.86	4.18
Recreation	1.07	1.32	1.07	0.92
Utilities	1.27	1.56	1.27	1.09
TOTAL COST PER UNIT	N.A.	$21.39	$17.39	$14.95

TABLE 20

Allocation of Non-Education Operating Expenditures to Hollymead Phase I Households on a Per Capita Basis

Function	Per Capita Cost	Single Family	Townhouse	Apartment
Law Inforcement	$ 1.77	$ 6.55	$ 5.66	$ 4.60
Fire Prevention	2.27	8.40	7.26	5.90
Health & Welfare*	1.33	4.92	4.26	3.46
General Government	11.75	43.48	37.60	30.55
Prison Care	0.61	2.26	1.95	1.59
Agriculture & Home Economics	0.78	2.89	2.50	2.03
TOTAL COST PER UNIT		$68.50	$59.23	$48.13

* 50% of total per capita expenditures for Health. Welfare is excluded.

TOTAL OPERATING EXPENDITURES ALLOCATED TO HOUSEHOLDS

Table 21 summarizes the above non-education operating expenditures plus operating expenditures for public education and shows the total allocated by dwelling type.

TABLE 21

Allocation of Operating Expenditures To Hollymead Phase I Households: Summary

Dwelling Type	Education	Other Functions*	TOTAL
Single Family	$508.00	$89.89	$597.89
Townhouse	435.49	76.62	512.11
Apartment	210.43	63.08	273.51

* From Tables 19 and 20.

ALLOCATION OF OPERATING EXPENDITURES FOR SERVICES USED BY BUSINESS ENTERPRISES

As noted in the General Methodology section at the beginning of Chapter Four, the share Hollymead business property represents of the total real property base in the County will be used in estimating business-linked operating expenditures for Hollymead Phase I. Thus, since Hollymead business enterprises represent 1.8 percent of the total real property value of the County, businesses will be allocated 1.8 percent of the current County operating expenditures for household/business-related items in the County budget--police protection, prison care, fire protection, general government, landfill, and utilities.

In addition to these public services, commercial and industrial enterprises place a considerable burden on local utilities, such as water and sewerage. This additional burden is offset to the extent that these services are paid by user charges, and therefore added utility costs do not affect the local operating budget.[71]

At present, the County's total real property tax revenues from industrial property total $153,000, or $37 per worker. Commercial enterprises planned for Hollymead Phase I will provide $51,041 in real property tax revenues, based on estimates provided by the developer. This would necessitate

---

71. The County is presently subsidizing the Albemarle Service Authority by providing a large interest-free loan.

TABLE 22

Operating Expenditures Allocated to Business Enterprises

Function	Amount
Law Enforcement	$1,447
Prison Care	437
Fire Protection	1,850
General Government	9,421
Landfill	1,044
Utilities	241
TOTAL	$14,440

approximately 766 new employees on the basis of fiscal 1972 tax revenues per employee.[72]

Unless the existing labor force is available within the County or within commuting distance of other jurisdictions,[73] these new enterprises are likely to attract new residents to the County. Prevailing wage rates in County's industrial and commercial enterprises indicate that the majority of workers could not afford most of the housing planned for Hollymead Phase I.

---

72. Albemarle County manufacturing industries are comparatively capital intensive. Value added per worker in 1967 was $15,300, compared to $12,176 for all Virginia manufacturing enterprises, as shown in the 1967 Census of Manufacturers--Virginia. Thus, the number of additional employees necessary to generate the property tax revenue is not unrealistic. This analysis excludes consideration of the secondary fiscal impact associated with new business enterprises. However, the implications for the public sector of projected industrial and commercial land-use requirements for the North Rivanna Community Cluster should be noted. See Appendix C.

73. This is unlikely on the basis of present employment levels.

To estimate the fiscal impact of new households attracted to the County by new business enterprises, the same methodology applied to determine costs and revenues from housing units (discussed in previous sections of this study) should be applied. Thus, given the wage structure of employees and their households, the likely demand for housing by type can be estimated.[74] The fiscal impact on the public sector would be estimated on the basis of income, household size, and type of housing unit likely to be occupied by new households. In the absence of data on the likely characteristics of the commercial enterprises to be located in Hollymead Phase I, such an analysis is not feasible as part of this study.

74. One approach to this analysis is discussed in F. James and J. Hughes, Economic Growth and Residential Patterns, (New Brunswick, N.J.: Center for Urban Policy Research, Rutgers--The State University, 1972).

CHAPTER FIVE
CAPITAL EXPENDITURE ESTIMATES: HOLLYMEAD PHASE I

GENERAL METHODOLOGY

Capital expenditure requirements are a crucial element in determining total costs associated with new development since, unless existing facilities are under-utilized, increases in population require new public and private sector capital investment. An alternative to such investment, given full utilization of facilities, would be a reduction in the level and quality of existing services, such as increased number of students in classrooms or double sessions, increased traffic congestion, or overcrowded recreational facilities.

In areas of rapid growth, public infrastructure investments frequently lag behind population increases because of public sector fiscal limitations, the initial diseconomies of scale associated with providing new facilities, or because of inadequate planning. As a result, there is usually at least a short-term degradation in the provision of public services.

The fiscal impact of increased capital expenditures on local government is often greater than the comparable impact of an increase in operating expenditures. This is because local government generally has to pay for many major capital expenditures such as schools, and police and fire stations, from its own resources while outlays to meet operating expenditures are frequently matched by the state and some cases by the federal government.[75] In estimating the capital needs of a community which is considering new development, capital expenditures include:

- School facilities directly linked with proposed new development;
- Other locally financed facilities directly linked with new development; and
- Facilities designed for use by the total population, including residents or business enterprises in proposed developments.

In the case of past capital expenditures, those linked to facilities fully utilized prior to new development, such as public schools, should not be considered as part of the capital cost attributable to the new development. Whether capital expenditures, which provide current as well as future benefits, should be paid from current revenues or over an extended time period, involves issues of equity, since the composition of the population using the capital improvements undergoes change during the useful life of the investment.[76]

LONG-TERM DEBT VS. PAY-AS-YOU-BUILD FINANCING

There are three methods of paying for major capital projects not funded from user charges: (1) the use of general revenues from current tax receipts; (2) the use of general obligation bonds; and (3) the use of <u>both</u> current revenue and general obligation bonds.[77] In the past, Albemarle

---

75. In Virginia, the State does not provide payment for school construction, although a loan fund is available.

76. For a theoretical discussion of public debt issues, see R. A. Musgrave, <u>The Theory of Public Finance</u> (New York: McGraw Hill Co., 1959).

77. Revenue bonds are those bonds secured with income received by a jurisdiction from the earnings of a revenue-producing interprise, such as waterworks. General obligation bonds are secured by an unconditional pledge of the jurisdiction's credit, including its taxing power.

County has chosen the first approach, and projections in this study will be made on the basis of the pattern and level of nonpublic-school expenditures in Albemarle County over the past few years. An alternative method, discussed in Appendix E, is to project long-range capital improvements and to estimate the general obligation which will be needed to pay for these projects.

The method of financing chosen by a jurisdiction influences the short and long term costs of capital investment. In a slow-growing jurisdiction, a substantial portion of capital needs are frequently paid from current revenues, on a "pay as you go" basis. Capital expenditures, such as those made for many utilities, are usually self-financing through revenue bonds, and thus impose no direct burden on the public sector fiscal structure. However, major capital costs, particularly in areas of rapid growth, cannot be financed from current funds. Therefore, general obligation bonds are issued for a selected payback period.

The existing capital improvement program for Albemarle County suggests a 20-year payback period,[78] while in its estimates for the North Rivanna project the County Planning Staff uses a 30-year period. The suggested approach for determining per annum cost involves calculating the straight line amortization of capital over the useful life of the investment and adding the interest on the average balance outstanding.[79]

A number of factors must be considered in determining the optimal bond repayment period. A shorter repayment period provides a jurisdiction

78. See, R. H. Payne, "Capital Improvement Plan for Albemarle County, 1970-2000," March 1971.

79. The formula is $A = P\frac{i(1 + i)^n}{(1 + i)^n - 1}$ where A is the per annum cost and P = total outlay.

with more flexibility in adopting long-range capital projects expansion plans. The annual cost per $1,000 debt at a 5 percent interest rate over 20 years is $80.20. Increasing the bond to a 30 year payback period reduces the annual cost to $65.05. Beyond 30 years, given the same 5 percent interest rate, the annual reductions are smaller. Thus, extending the repayment period to 50 years only reduced the annual cost to $54.80. An additional disadvantage of longer term bonds is that they tend to carry higher interest rates, since the bond market discounts for anticipated inflation and uncertainty. As a result, there is pressure on local government to reduce the length of the payback period.

For the purposes of this study, an interest rate of 5 percent and separate calculations using _both_ 20 and 30 year bond repayment periods will be made in computing the fiscal impact of Hollymead Phase I.

THE USEFUL ECONOMIC LIFE OF THE INVESTMENT

An alternative approach for computing the capital cost would be to estimate the useful economic life of the investment (excluding the value of the land), independent of the bond repayment period.[80] Presumably, if the actual economic life could be estimated, the annual interest charges on a bond could be added to the amortized per annum economic life of the project. Thus, if bonds for a project had a 30-year repayment period, but the economic life of the project was 40 years, the annual capital costs could be reduced, although the difference would not be substantial. Technological and other changes may result in a shorter useful economic

80. A preliminary attempt at this is noted in W. Isard and R. Coughlin, _op. cit._

life for a capital investment than initially projected.[81] In addition, elements of a particular project are likely to have differing economic life spans. As a result, basing estimates on the anticipated economic life of a project has practical limitations.

ECONOMIES AND DISECONOMIES OF SCALE

Population growth may result in necessitating capital investments which have higher incremental costs compared to average costs, as may be the case in sewerage treatment plants and certain utilities. While the necessity for a capital investment (such as tertiary sewerage treatment plants) may be triggered by identifiable land-use change, the present practice in most communities is to distribute the cost among all taxpayers, new and old.[82]

In other capital projects, there may be economies of scale. For example, the per pupil cost of a high school designed for 500 students are substantially higher than those for a school designed for 2,000 students, given the same level of facilities.[83] It is not feasible to make a satisfactory projection of capital costs when a land-use change involving

81. For example, many comparatively new school buildings are undergoing major renovation to adapt the structure to the "open classroom" concept, a recent innovation in education.

82. In general, capital outlays financed from general revenue bonds are part of the local budget, and are repaid from general tax revenues. That is, most jurisdictions allocate the cost of a new facility to the total community rather than to just the residents of the area which has caused the need for new capital expenditures. Certain jurisdictions have special taxing districts, where the repayment of capital outlays is allocated only to the area which utilizes the facilities. The likely users of most new facilities such as sewers or schools can usually be identified, although in some instances, such as transportation facilities, the user group is likely to extend beyond those who necessitated the capital outlay.

83. W. Isard and R. Coughlin, *op. cit.*

few housing units or small commercial developments is anticipated, since the incremental capital costs are step functions rather than continuous functions.[84]

Finally, it should be noted that for the purpose of these estimates, an assumption is made regarding the allocation of capital expenditures to Hollymead Phase I. Estimates of capital expenditures for the development were made by the County Planning Department based on the projected needs of the entire North Rivanna Community Cluster, rather than by sub-division. Since more detailed data are not available on the specific needs of Hollymead Phase I, diseconomies of scale are not considered. It will be assumed that capital expenditures associated with supplying facilities to the North Rivanna Community Cluster can be applied proportionately to Hollymead Phase I without affecting unit costs.

Allocation of capital expenditures for facilities used by both households and business enterprises is based on the share each represents of the total market value in the entire Cluster; i.e., 78.3 percent will be allocated to households and 22.7 percent to business enterprises. This is the same proportion as in Hollymead Phase I.

CAPITAL EXPENDITURES ALLOCATED TO HOUSEHOLDS IN HOLLYMEAD PHASE I

EDUCATION

Estimates of capital expenditures for education directly linked to development are discussed in this section. Projected expenditures are converted into per student or per capita unit costs, as appropriate. Public

---

84. Fortunately, the total North Rivanna Cluster is sufficiently large to estimate its impact on a number of capital projects.

school capital expenditures are based on the mean cost of construction for elementary, intermediate and secondary schools for the North Rivanna Community Cluster as estimated by the Albemarle County Planning Department. In Table 23, these values are compared to per student costs in the Fairfax County, Virginia[85] budget as a check to determine whether the values are within a reasonable range.

TABLE 23

Fiscal 1972 Capital Expenditures Per Student--Albemarle County As Compared with Fairfax County

	Capacity		Cost Per Student	
	Albemarle	Fairfax	Albemarle	Fairfax
Elementary	800	660	$2,034	$2,333
Intermediate	1,200	1,400	2,333	3,843
Secondary	1,200	2,400	4,500*	4,263
Weighted Mean Cost Per Student	N.A.	N.A.	$2,669	$3,104

* Albemarle County estimates $5,000 per student.

In the absence of detailed demographic data, it will be assumed that the probability of attending elementary schools as compared to secondary schools is independent of the type of residential structure. It is likely, however, that there is a higher probability of students attending elementary

85. Fairfax County Department of Finance, "Fairfax County Budget For Fiscal 1972," Fairfax County, Va., 1972.

schools who reside in apartments compared to single-family units.[86] Thus, since capital expenditures for elementary schools are lower, per student capital (as well as operating) expenditures would be lower for those residing in apartments.

A comparison of Fairfax and Albemarle Counties indicates higher elementary and intermediate school costs in Fairfax County, but lower high school costs. The difference in high school unit cost may be associated with economies of scale when capacity is doubled. Construction costs in Fairfax County may also be somewhat above the Albemarle County level. As an average cost, the $2,669 per student Albemarle County estimate appears reasonable.

Table 24 shows capital costs per student for Hollymead Phase I, as estimated by the Albemarle County Planning Department.[87]

TABLE 24

Capital Expenditures Per Student in Hollymead Phase I

Dwelling Type	(ADM) Per Unit	Student Cost	Ammortized Cost Per Annum	
			20 Year Bond	30 Year Bond
Single Family	1.05	$2,802	$224.72	$182.27
Townhouse	0.90	2,402	192.64	156.25
Apartment	0.43	1,148	92.07	74.68
Weighted Mean	0.85	$2,265	$181.60	$143.50

86. In a suburban area of New Jersey, 90 percent of all students from apartments were in grades K to 9, only 10 percent in grades 10 to 12, see G. Sterlieb, op. cit. In 1971, the cost of salaries per elementary school student in Albemarle County was $372, secondary student $548, or a 47.2 percent difference.

87. County high school construction cost estimates have been reduced from $6 million to $5.4 million.

In determining the capital cost per student for elementary schools, an adjustment has been made to reflect the contribution by the builder of 37 acres of land valued at $74,000.[88] The amount represents 4.3 percent of the total estimated cost of an elementary school. As a result, the per student cost is reduced from $2,125 to $2,034; per student school construction costs are based on capacity utilization of each school.

An alternative approach, not applied to this study, would be to assume that present facilities are being utilized to capacity and therefore new capital costs should be fully charged to the development (or part of the development) which "triggered" the demand for the new facility, until such time as the new facility is fully utilized.

RECREATION

The County Planning Office estimates an initial capital investment of $500,000 to provide 75 acres of parks for the projected population of 18,000

TABLE 25

Capital Expenditures for Recreation--
Hollymead Phase I

Dwelling Type	Total Cost Per Unit	Amortized Cost Per Annum	
		20 Year Bond	30 Year Bond
Single Family	$105.67	$8.43	$6.87
Townhouse	90.29	7.21	5.87
Apartment	77.65	6.21	5.05

88. This is based on an estimated market value of $2,000 per acre prior to rezoning or subdivision.

in the North Rivanna Community Cluster.[89] Capital expenditures for recreation allocated to residents in Hollymead Phase I on the basis of household income are shown in Table 25.[90]

GOVERNMENT SERVICES SUBSTATION

The total cost for the government services substation which is to utilize six acres and will include health, library and public safety facilities, is estimated at $600,000. Since the cost is allocated between households and business enterprises in the North Rivanna Community Cluster in proportion to their market value, 78 percent of the total cost of the complex ($468,000) should be allocated among households in the Cluster.

The County Planning office does not break down the cost of the substation facility by function. As noted previously, certain functions provided within the substation will vary with the income of the new residents, however, because of the mix of services provided, costs will be allocated on a per capita basis. The per annum costs are shown in Table 26. The per capita cost for the facility

TABLE 26

Capital Expenditures for Governmental Services Substation--Hollymead Phase I

Dwelling Type	Total Cost Per Unit	Amortized Cost Per Annum	
		20 Year Bond	30 Year Bond
Single Family	$96.20	$7.72	$6.25
Townhouse	83.20	6.67	5.41
Apartment	67.60	4.11	4.40

89. Albemarle County Department of Planning, Staff Report: Hollymead, op. cit.

90. Although 20 and 30 year bond repayment periods are shown, the value of land (as distinct from improvements) should not be depreciated, although the initial outlay for the land must be amortized.

(based on 18,000 residents) is $26.00. It is assumed that increasing the County population by almost 50 percent will not require additional new public facilities, such as those utilized by general government.

LANDFILL SITE

The cost of acquiring a landfill site (for refuse disposal) is estimated at $75,000. Of this total, 78 percent or $58,500 is allocated to households on the basis of household income, the balance to business enterprises.

Table 27 shows landfill costs.

TABLE 27

Capital Expenditures for Landfill--
Hollymead Phase I

Dwelling Type	Total Cost Per Unit	Amortized Cost Per Annum	
		20 Year Bond	30 Year Bond
Single Family	$13.20	$1.06	$0.86
Townhouse	10.56	0.85	0.69
Apartment	9.34	0.75	0.61

HOSPITALS

The County Planning Office staff has identified the need for nine additional hospital beds per 1,000 population, or 162 beds for the total North Rivanna complex; unfortunately, no cost estimates are provided. Fairfax County estimates that three hospital beds are required per 1,000 persons, with a total cost of $45,000 per bed. Using Fairfax County values as a proxy, the total hospital capital expenditure (only partially funded from local resources) required would be over $2 million.

At present, the University of Virginia hospital provides its facilities to County residents. It will be assumed that the State government, by expansion of the University medical facilities, will continue to provide hospital facilities to Albemarle County.[91]

TOTAL CAPITAL COSTS PER HOUSEHOLD

Costs per dwelling type for capital outlays linked directly to the proposed development are shown in Table 28.

TABLE 28

Capital Expenditures--Households in Hollymead Phase I

Function	Single Family		Townhouse		Apartment	
	20 Year Bond	30 Year Bond	20 Year Bond	30 Year Bond	20 Year Bond	30 Year Bond
Education (Primary and Secondary)	$224.72	$182.27	$192.64	$156.25	$ 92.07	$ 74.68
Recreation	8.43	6.87	7.21	5.87	6.21	5.05
Government Services Substation	7.72	6.25	6.67	5.41	4.11	4.40
Landfill	1.06	0.86	0.85	0.69	0.75	0.61
TOTAL	$241.93	$196.25	$207.37	$168.22	$103.14	$ 84.74

CAPITAL EXPENDITURES ALLOCATED TO EXISTING AND NEW HOUSEHOLDS IN THE COUNTY

The previous section identified capital projects linked directly with the proposed development. However, there are additional capital projects

91. This is reflected in higher State costs, as shown in Appendix B.

designed to serve the entire County, rather than a specific area. The capital projects discussed below do not appear to be directly linked to a specific development; however, they are in part linked with recent and projected increases in population which are the result of land-use changes made by County officials and in part they reflect past demand. If it could be determined that certain projects were initiated exclusively as a result of new growth, the capital costs linked to Hollymead would be higher. Since County reports do not discuss assumptions regarding the level of future population growth used in determining the size of the project, it is not feasible to isolate the incremental costs associated with a growth in population.

CAPITAL EXPENDITURES FINANCED FROM CURRENT REVENUES

In Albemarle County, most non-education capital outlays have been paid from current revenues. As a result, debt service obligations (with the exception of school construction bonds) are limited.

Table 29 shows capital expenditure items which appear in the 1972 budget for Albemarle County. Elementary and secondary school construction projects, which were discussed earlier, have been excluded. Although not all funds appropriated for fiscal 1972 have been spent, this represents only a postponement of expenditures.

Watershed, airport and jail costs can be allocated between households and business enterprises, while education and recreation costs should be allocated to households only. If the County plans to continue to meet capital needs on a "pay as you go" basis, an estimated $1,134,730 in

TABLE 29

Albemarle County Capital Expenditures, Fiscal 1972

Function*	Appropriation
Watershed projects	$ 614,996
Joint airport improvement	100,000
County jail	79,880
Community college	185,570
Vocational--technical center	75,000
Chris Green Recreation Center	47,120
Mint Spring Recreation Center	32,164
TOTAL	$1,134,730

*Excluding elementary and secondary education. Although $317,136 is appropriated by the County for these recreation centers, it is anticipated that federal grants will cover 75 percent of the cost.

capital costs will be incurred by the County during fiscal 1972,[92] which can be allocated among households ($1,041,730) and business enterprises ($93,000). Annual per capita costs are $22.48.[93] (Costs will be allocated on a per capita basis, although the demand for certain projects may vary with residents' income.)

Table 30 shows how capital expenditures paid from current revenues are allocated to households in Hollymead Phase I by dwelling type.

---

92. 1971-72 appropriation, less recreational facilities. This assumes that the level of capital expenditures to be paid from current revenues will average $1 million.

93. Based on a population of 40,000 in 1972 and 2,662 potential Hollymead Phase I residents.

TABLE 30

Allocation of Capital Expenditures
To Households in Hollymead Phase I
Financed from Current Revenues

Dwelling Type	Density Per Unit	Cost Per Unit
Single Family	3.7	$83.18
Townhouse	3.2	71.94
Apartment	2.6	58.45

CAPITAL EXPENDITURES FINANCED FROM CURRENT REVENUE AND GENERAL OBLIGATION BONDS

An alternative strategy for the County is to meet part of its capital needs (other than for public schools) from current revenues, with the remainder financed from general obligation bonds. It will be assumed that the County will allocate 10 percent of its current revenue for capital expenditures (approximately the actual share allocated in the past decade). For fiscal 1972, this would total $657,000 for capital projects not associated with new development.

It will also be assumed that half the capital outlay will be for projects utilized jointly by households and business enterprises--the balance utilized by households only. Since existing business property represents 11.7 percent of the market value for all real property in the County, $38,494 will be allocated to existing and new business enterprises, $618,566 to households.

In addition, $800,000 per annum (in constant 1971 dollars) in general obligation bonds will be obtained to finance projects not paid for by revenue bonds or State and federal funds. For the purpose of this analysis, capital expenditures will include only those to be made over the next five years. Thus, a total of $4 million will be borrowed via 20 or 30 year general obligation bonds over the next five years. It is recognized that after 1977, additional capital outlays will be necessitated, prior to repayment of earlier bonds. However, in view of the limited data on future capital needs (see Appendix E), these future costs will not be considered.

Dividing $4 million in capital outlays between payments from current revenue and through borrowing,[94] and allocating them between households and business (as noted previously), cost per dwelling unit for households in Hollymead Phase I are shown in Table 31. The total household share will be

TABLE 31

Allocation of Capital Expenditures Financed From Current Revenue and General Obligation Bonds to Households in Hollymead Phase I

Dwelling Type	Capital Expenditures Financed Current Revenue	Annual Amortized Cost for Capital Expenditure		Total Capital Expenditure	
		20 Year Bonds	30 Year Bonds	20 Year Bonds	30 Year Bonds
Single Family	$53.72	$26.16	$21.26	$79.88	$74.98
Townhouse	46.46	22.64	18.39	69.10	64.85
Apartment	37.75	18.40	14.95	56.15	52.70

$3.77 million, or $88.49 per capita. The balance, or $0.23 million is allocated to business enterprises.

94. On the basis of discussion with County officials and past fiscal trends in the County, it appears that the division of payment for capital projects is the most likely policy to be followed by the County in the coming year.

CAPITAL EXPENDITURES ALLOCATED TO BUSINESS ENTERPRISES

Capital expenditures allocated to business enterprises include: (1) those directly associated with business enterprises in the development and (2) those associated with all business enterprises in the County (business enterprises in the development and those existing in the balance of the County).

CAPITAL EXPENDITURES ALLOCATED TO HOLLYMEAD PHASE I BUSINESS ENTERPRISES

The commercial development in Hollymead Phase I comprises 9.5 percent of the total commercial and industrial real property value in North Rivanna. Table 32 shows the allocation of costs on this basis.

TABLE 32

Allocation of Capital Expenditures to Business Enterprises in Hollymead Phase I

Function	Total Capital Expenditure	Hollymead Phase I	Per Annum Cost 20 Year Bond	Per Annum Cost 30 Year Bond
Government Services	$132,000	$12,540	$1,003	$815
Substation Landfill	16,500	1,567	125	102
TOTAL	$148,500	$14,107	$1,128	$917

CAPITAL EXPENDITURES ALLOCATED TO EXISTING AND NEW COUNTY BUSINESS ENTERPRISES

The proposed business enterprises in Hollymead Phase I have an estimated real property market value of $6.5 million. The present market value of existing commercial and industrial property is $50.5 million. Thus, if the Hollymead commercial development is built, its value of $6.5 million represents approximately 11 percent of the County's total business property, including the new development. Therefore, 11 percent of the capital outlay linked to business enterprises will be allocated to Hollymead Phase I.

Table 33 shows the allocation of capital expenditures to existing business enterprises in the balance of the County and to those in Hollymead Phase I.

TABLE 33

Allocation of Capital Expenditures to New and Existing Business Enterprises

	From Current Revenues	Per Annum Cost 20 Year Bond	Per Annum Cost 30 Year Bond
Capital Expenditures Allocated to New and Existing Business	$38,434	$18,400	$14,950
Capital Expenditures Allocated to Business in Hollymead Phase I	4,228	1,932	1,570

CHAPTER SIX
FINDINGS AND POLICY ALTERNATIVES

REVENUE-EXPENDITURE SUMMARY

REVENUES

Column (1) of Table 34 shows annual revenues which will accrue to the County from Hollymead Phase I. Total revenues less revenue from existing land use[95] yields a net total of $503,099 in revenues accruing to Albemarle County from Hollymead Phase I.

OPERATING EXPENDITURES

As shown in column (2) of Table 34, total annual operating expenditures associated with Hollymead Phase I are $414,013. Examination of the revenue-operating expenditure flow indicates that single family homes yield an annual surplus of $45 per unit, apartments, a $73 surplus, while townhouses show an annual deficit of $11 per unit. Since business enterprises incur only 3.5 percent of total operating expenditures, and account for 15.6 percent of revenues, they show a substantial surplus.

CAPITAL EXPENDITURES LINKED TO HOLLYMEAD PHASE I

Column (3) of Table 34 shows annual capital outlays associated with Hollymead Phase I are between $131,102 and $161,323, depending on the

95. See Chapter Three for estimate of revenue from existing land use.

TABLE 34

Hollymead Phase I: Total Annual Revenue-Expenditure Summary

		(1)		(2)		Capital Expenditures[a] (3) Hollymead-Linked				(4) Entire County			
	No. Units	Revenue Per Unit	Total Revenue	Operating Expenditures Per Unit	Total Operating Expenditures	Cost Per Unit 20-Year	Cost Per Unit 30-Year	Total Cost 20-Year	Total Cost 30-Year	Cost Per Unit 20-Year	Cost Per Unit 30-Year	Total Cost 20-Year	Total Cost 30-Year
Single Family	358	$643.24	$230,280	$597.89	$214,045	$241.93	$196.25	$ 86,611	$ 70,258	$79.88	$74.88	$28,597	$26,843
Townhouse	256	501.56	128,399	512.11	131,100	207.37	168.22	53,087	43,064	69.10	64.85	17,690	16,601
Apartment	199	346.62	68,977	273.51	54,428	103.14	84.74	20,497	16,863	56.15	52.70	11,174	10,487
Business Enterprises	N.A.	N.A.	78,792	N.A.	14,440	N.A.	N.A.	1,128	917	N.A.	N.A.	6,160	5,798
Subtotal			$506,448		$414,013			$161,323	$131,101			$63,621	$59,729
Existing Land Use	N.A.	N.A.	$ 3,349		N.A.	N.A.	N.A.	N.A.	N.A.	N.A.	N.A.	N.A.	N.A.
TOTAL PER ANNUM			$503,099		$414,013			$161,323	$131,101			$63,621	$59,729

TOTAL ANNUAL REVENUES = $503,099

TOTAL ANNUAL EXPENDITURES[b] = $414,013 + $131,101 + $59,729 = $604,844

a. 5 percent bonds.
b. 30-year bonds.

length of the bond repayment period. Using the 30-year period,[96] the combined (operating and capital) Hollymead Phase I-linked expenditure total of $545,114 annually exceeds net revenues ($503,099) by about 8 percent. This deficit is due to the impact of single family dwellings and townhouses. Apartments almost "break even," while business enterprises continue to show a substantial surplus. The use of 20-year bonds increases capital expenditures by an additional $30,222 each year.

CAPITAL EXPENDITURES ASSOCIATED WITH THE ENTIRE COUNTY

As noted in the previous section of this study, the level of County capital expenditures over the next five years can only be estimated. In addition, the degree to which Hollymead Phase I residents and businesses increase the demand for certain County facilities cannot be determined with any precision. For example, the addition of 20,000 new residents (the total North Rivanna Community Cluster) is likely to necessitate the expansion of general government facilities, while the addition of a development of fewer than 3,000 new residents (i.e., Hollymead Phase I) is not likely to have a similar effect. Thus, the fiscal impact of Hollymead Phase I on annual capital expenditures in Albemarle County has been estimated on the basis of a proportionate share of expenditures resulting from the total North Rivanna Community Cluster. As shown in Table 34, the capital expenditures linked to the entire County are $59,729. This results in total County expenditures of $604,844

---

96. 30-year bonds are a better approximation of the economic life of an investment than are 20-year bonds.

FISCAL FLOW SUMMARY

The totals per annum in Table 34 show that the difference between total revenues ($503,099) and expenditures for Hollymead Phase I, given 30-year bond repayment periods for capital outlays, is $101,745 per annum. Without the proposed commercial development in the project, the difference between revenues and expenditures would be increased by more than $50,000 each year. The causes for and implications of this gap are discussed below.

The net deficit per housing unit is estimated in Table 35. The annual surplus of $57,637 from business enterprises (the difference for business enterprise between columns (1) and (2)-(4) in Table 34) is allocated among dwelling units on a per capita basis as follows:

TABLE 35

Net Deficit Per Annum For Dwelling Units in Hollymead Phase I

Dwelling Type	Deficit Per Annum	Commercial Surplus Allocation	Annual Net Deficit Per Unit
Single Family	$226	$81	$145
Townhouse	244	70	174
Apartment	64	57	7
Weighted Mean	$191	$72	$119

The deficit can be absorbed by the households and business enterprises in the County, or it could be offset by a cash payment from the developer.

For example, in the case of single family houses, the County would have to receive a cash payment of $1,535 per unit which would provide $145 annually to the County for 20 years.[97] This cash payment represents 4.3 percent of the mean market value of single family homes in Hollymead Phase I. To provide this sum for a 30 year period, a cash payment of $1,799 would be required. (The length of the developer's repayment period should be linked to the length of the bonds issued by the County for capital outlays necessitated by the development.)

A total payment to the County of $1,040,640, or an average of $1,280 per housing unit would be necessary to offset the total 20-year deficit resulting from all dwelling units in Hollymead Phase I.

FINDINGS

The results of this study indicate that given the present tax structure from a <u>public sector</u> fiscal viewpoint, Hollymead Phase I, and, unless present plans are revised, all sub-divisions of the North Rivanna Community Cluster, is likely to be a liability to the County. This fiscal liability is primarily due to the large capital outlays necessitated by having to provide public services to a substantial increase in population in an area of the County where the infrastructure is not developed. Total County per student expenditures, the largest item in the budget, are estimated at $476.06 for operating costs and $173.48 for capital expenditures (30-year

---

97. The formula used to determine cash payment is: the present value of an annuity = $\frac{[1 - (1 + i)^n]}{i}$, where n = 20 or 30 years, and i = 7 percent. The use of the 7 percent interest rate reflects the current rate of return on a long-term non-risk investment. The lower 5 percent rate on County bonds reflects their tax-exempt status.

bond repayment) or a total of $749.54. The average education expenditure for all Hollymead Phase I households (single family, townhouse and apartment) is a total of $547.70 for operating and capital costs.

The fiscal liability is attributable to capital outlays necessitated by the Hollymead Development for facilities, such as schools, which are either presently unavailable or fully utilized. Operating expenditures are met by revenues generated from the development.

Legislation which has focused on the issue of development has cited the need for capital expenditures as justification for granting long-term delays in housing construction, or alternatively, requiring the developer to pay the difference between the cost of providing new facilities and the revenue generated by the development. Although the State of Virginia shares the operating costs for education, public safety and general government, it does not provide any funds to offset capital outlays. Hence, the full weight of increased capital costs resulting from a development must fall on the County government.

It is also assumed that the business enterprises will occupy the large areas the developers have allocated for commerce and industry concurrently with residents of the development, although it is recognized that the secondary impact of such large scale development, resulting in a greatly expanded labor force, requires consideration. To yield a fiscal surplus, the wage structure of new private enterprises would have to be above present levels. For a determination of both the primary and secondary impact of the total Community Cluster, additional data would have to be analyzed.

POLICY ALTERNATIVES

To reduce the likely negative fiscal impact on the County of Hollymead Phase I, a number of alternatives can be suggested. Since capital expenditures and particularly school construction costs are pivotal, new residential development could be channeled into areas of the County where existing schools are likely to be underutilized as the population matures. However, this alternative may present additional problems, including the lack of legal and administrative tools to implement such a policy, the cost of land available for large scale development in these areas, the demand for comparatively expensive homes in what might be less desirable sections of the County, and related factors.

Another possible alternative would be to require that developers contributed to the cost of providing capital facilities as is now being required of developers in Loudoun County, Virginia. As shown in Table 34 and the related text, in the case of Hollymead Phase I this would amount to a total of $1,040,640 to offset the total 20-year deficit for all housing units in Hollymead Phase I.

Another alternative, which is beyond the power of the County, is for the State government, which is likely to benefit from new growth (see Appendix B), to pay part or all of the capital expenditures incurred. At present, the State government pays only for highways, and the level of this payment is only partially related to growth.

As noted earlier, there are other economic and non-economic issues which should be considered in decisions regarding land use. These factors are briefly noted in Appendix F. Appendix G presents a discussion of data sources for fiscal impact analyses.

APPENDIX A
SELECTED DEMOGRAPHIC AND SOCIOECONOMIC CHARACTERISTICS OF NEW COMMUNITIES WITHIN ALBEMARLE COUNTY

As a supplement to the general profiles of Albemarle County discussed in Chapter One, this Appendix presents detailed data on the residential areas within the County. The major objective is to determine whether there are areas in the County which have demographic and socioeconomic characteristics similar to the Hollymead Development.

For established Standard Metropolitan Statistical Areas (SMSA's),[1] intra-County data are published by the Census Bureau. Because Albemarle County is not included in an SMSA, intra-County data had to be extracted from Census computer tapes by magisterial district.[2]

INCOME DISTRIBUTION

As shown in Table A-1, the proportion of families with moderate and high incomes varies sharply among districts. In two district--Charlottesville and Ivy--58 percent of families earned over $10,000.[3] In the Ivy district, 16.5 percent of all families earned above $25,000. In contrast, less than 30 percent of the families in the Scottsville and S. Miller

---

1. By definition, an SMSA is a county or group of contiguous counties or "twin cities" with a combined population of at least 50,000.

2. The magisterial district boundaries defined by the Bureau of the Census for the 1970 Census of Population and Housing have changed. The data analysis is based on the earlier boundaries.

3. All data are based on 1969 incomes. Income has risen about 22 percent between 1969 and 1972.

TABLE A-1

Family Income Distribution By District

District	No. of Families	Family Income				
		Less Than $10,000	$10,000-$14,999	$15,000-$24,999	$25,000-$49,999	$50,000 and over
Charlottesville	3,056	41.2	25.9	22.3	8.8	1.8
Ivy	674	41.7	25.0	16.8	12.0	4.5
Rivanna	1,549	58.8	27.9	10.4	2.4	0.5
White Hall	1,240	63.1	24.2	10.6	2.1	0.0
Scottsville	1,141	71.4	18.3	7.0	2.2	1.1
S. Miller	1,227	70.2	22.3	5.4	1.7	0.4

districts earned over $10,000. The mean income in Ivy is estimated at $16,800, or more than 70 percent above the County mean.

COST OF HOUSING

The distribution of owner-occupied dwelling units by value is shown in Table A-2. As expected, house values follow the same pattern as income. In the affluent Ivy district, 75.6 percent of all units are valued at above $20,000, and 37.3 percent above $50,000. However, in Scottsville, which has the highest share of low and moderate income families, only 15.2 percent of all owner occupied units are valued at above $20,000, only 2.2 percent above $35,000.

TABLE A-2

Distribution of House Value for Owner-Occupied Units

District	No. of Units	Owner-Occupied House Value: Less Than $20,000	$20,000-$24,999	$25,000-$34,999	$35,000-$49,999	$50,000 and over
Charlottesville	1,521	18.4	8.6	24.2	33.7	15.1
Ivy	402	24.4	5.5	15.4	17.4	37.3
Rivanna	660	49.3	17.0	19.8	9.7	4.2
White Hall	521	66.7	18.0	10.4	3.8	1.1
Scottsville	498	84.8	7.2	5.8	0.8	1.4
S. Miller	519	72.1	17.0	4.2	2.3	4.4

DEMOGRAPHIC CHARACTERISTICS OF HOUSING OCCUPANTS

In the affluent Ivy district, owner-occupied households consist primarily of middle-aged residents: 61 percent of the residents in owner-occupied units are over 45 years old; and 19 percent are over 65 years of age. However, 44 percent of the residents living in rental units were under 30 years of age; only 27 percent over 45 years of age. In the Scottsville district, the same pattern holds, with 70 percent of owner-occupied households headed by persons over 45 years old. The pattern in all areas of Albemarle County, including areas with few college students, follows the national trend--homeowners tend to be older, and renters younger, than the community average.

PRIMARY AND SECONDARY EDUCATION

As shown in Table A-3, approximately 92 percent of all students in the County attend public schools. In higher income areas, as in the Ivy district,

TABLE A-3

Distribution of Public and Private School Students by District

District	Elementary		High School		College	
	Public	Private	Public	Private	Public	Private
Charlottesville	1,665	219	572	85	3,486	216
Ivy	373	136	114	56	143	12
Rivanna	1,020	45	395	55	142	27
White Hall	997	44	247	--	5	--
Scottsville	763	16	314	--	12	32
S. Miller	907	18	363	12	78	9
TOTAL	5,725	478	2,005	208	3,866	298

28 percent of the students attend private schools, while in Scottsville only one percent are enrolled in private school. Elementary school enrollment as a percent of total public school enrollment varies slightly, from 69.8 percent in Scottsville to 74.9 percent in Ivy.

HIGHER EDUCATION

Census data indicate that 3,702 of the total 4,164 college students in the County reside in the Charlottesville district.[4] In other districts of the County the proportion of college students does not deviate sharply from that in counties in the balance of the State. In the lower income White Hall and Scottsville districts, there are only a total of 49 college students,

4. Since college students are concentrated in the Charlottesville district, it is feasible to adjust Census higher education data for the County which were taken prior to the annexation by the City of a portion of the County.

compared to 561 high school students; the proportion of college students is considerably higher in the Ivy district.

FINDINGS

This brief examination of selected demographic and socioeconomic characteristics of the districts within Albemarle County indicates that the County is not a homogeneous area. Furthermore, no specific area within the County can be identified which closely resembles the likely characteristics of the Hollymead Phase I development. This finding may have implications for several of the policy alternatives suggested in Chapter Six.

APPENDIX B
THE IMPACT OF THE HOLLYMEAD DEVELOPMENT ON THE STATE GOVERNMENT

The fiscal impact of Hollymead Phase I on the State of Virginia should be considered from both the revenue and expenditure perspective. As in the County fiscal impact analysis, State revenues and expenditures resulting from residential and business development will be considered.

STATE REVENUES

STATE REVENUE SOURCES

Table B-1 shows major State revenue sources. More than 90 percent of the total revenue comes from households within the State.

TABLE B-1

State Revenues--General Fund (1971-1972)*

Tax Source	Percent of Fund
Individual Income	43.2
State Sales and Use	30.6
Corporate Income	7.0
Insurance Company Premiums	3.5
Alcohol, Beer and Tobacco	4.8
Inheritance, Wills	2.9
Other	7.7
TOTAL	100.0

*Division of the Budget, Analysis of Appropriations and Revenues 1970-1972 Biennum, Richmond, Va., December 1970

With the exception of taxes paid by business enterprises, State taxes vary with household income. As a result, State taxes are directly linked to the income of residents.[1]

STATE REVENUES--CHANGE IN RESIDENCE

The previous residence of those relocating in a new development can have a considerable effect on the fiscal impact of the development.

State revenues from residents who relocate to more expensive housing within the County, without a change in income, are likely to pay somewhat less in State taxes. If such a household purchases a new dwelling unit, the household is likely to allocate a higher share of its income for taxes and mortgage interest, thus reducing taxable personal income. Increased consumption of housing (either owned or rented) without a change in income also results in less disposable income for purchases subject to State sales and other excise taxes.

State revenues from households who have migrated to Albemarle County from other parts of Virginia will also be essentially unaffected unless household income changes as a result of the move, or the share of household income allocated for housing is altered. Since the State does not derive revenue from residential property, a change in the value of property owned or rented directly affects local but not State revenues. Between 1965-1970 about 34 percent of those changing household locations in Albemarle County were residents of Virginia, but not of the County.

Revenues from out-of-state migrants (who comprised 31 percent of those who changed household locations between 1965-1970) must be computed on the

1. The rate of change depends on the tax. Personal income taxes rise more rapidly than income (elasticity is greater than 1.0) while sales taxes do not rise as rapidly as income (elasticity is less than 1.0).

basis of the demographic and socioeconomic characteristics of the new households. Since these residents, regardless of their income, did not pay Virginia taxes previously, total State revenues based on household characteristics must be derived.

STATE REVENUES FROM HOUSEHOLDS IN HOLLYMEAD PHASE I

STATE INCOME TAX

Estimated State income tax payments from Hollymead residents are contained in Table B-2.[2]

TABLE B-2

State Income Tax Payments--Hollymead Phase I Households

Dwelling Type*	Total Income	Taxable Income	Tax Per Household	Tax Per Capita
Single Family	$18,637	$12,627	$501	$135
Townhouse	12,750	7,990	319	100
Apartments	9,231	6,158	178	68
Mean	$14,460	$ 9,580	$374	$107

*It is again assumed that single-family dwellings and townhouses will be owner-occupied, and apartments will be renter occupied.

Albemarle County residents' personal income tax payments are higher than the State average; $68 per capita compared to the State average of

2. It is assumed that interest and property taxes on owner occupied dwellings (townhouses and single family) are deducted to determine taxable income. Tax rates in effect in fiscal 1972 are applied.

$55 in fiscal 1970.[3] As Table B-2 shows, mean per capita tax payments by Hollymead residents ($107) would be 35 percent, which is above the average projected fiscal 1972 level of $79 per capita.[4]

STATE SALES TAX

The State sales tax is the second major general revenue source. The anticipated collection for 1971-1972 is $54 per capita. Of this total, $36 goes to the State general fund, with the balance redistributed to local government.

TABLE B-3

State Sales Tax Collections--
Hollymead Phase I Households

Dwelling Type	Estimated Income	Sales Tax as Percent of Income	Sales Tax Collections	Per Capita
Single Family	$18,637	1.23%	$229	$62
Townhouse	12,750	1.35	172	54
Apartment	9,231	1.44	133	50
Weighted Mean	$14,460	1.32%	$187	$57

As shown in Table B-3, mean per capita sales tax receipts ($57) would be 6 percent above the State per capita mean. Of this total, one-third, or $19 would redistributed to local governments in the State.

3. This is due to 1.2 percent of families with an income of over $50,000, more than twice the State average.

4. J. L. Knapp, "Fiscal Prospects and Alternatives," Commonwealth of Virginia Division of State Planning, April 1971, p. 101. These State income tax projections appear conservative.

OTHER REVENUES

Other State revenues, such as insurance premiums, tax purchases of alcohol, beer, tobacco, and inheritance taxes, can be expected to increase as income rises. It will be assumed, as with sales taxes, that the increase will be 6 percent above the State average, or $47 per capita. These revenue sources total $206.9 million in fiscal 1972, or $44 per capita.

TOTAL REVENUES

Total State revenues from Hollymead Phase I residents, as presented in Table B-4, can be expected to be somewhat higher than the State mean. It is estimated that one-third of all new residents are expected to be from out-of-State; the balance of residents would presumably pay approximately the same State taxes regardless of the location of their residence within Virginia. The estimated total revenues per household in Hollymead Phase I would be $550 from income and sales taxes. Other taxes ($207 million excluding corporate income) are estimated to follow the sales tax trend,

TABLE B-4

Total State Revenues From Households In Hollymead Phase I

Dwelling Type	Income Tax	Sales Tax	All Other Taxes	TOTAL
Single Family	$501	$229	$189	$919
Townhouse	319	172	144	635
Apartment	178	133	111	422
Weighted Mean	$364	$186	$156	$706

being 6 percent above the State average.[5] This would total $47 per capita in State revenues or $154 for each Hollymead Phase I household.

STATE REVENUES FROM BUSINESS ENTERPRISES

The major State revenue source (other than public service corporations) derived from the business sector is the corporate income tax. In view of the limited data on the proposed commercial development in Hollymead Phase I, it is not feasible to even crudely estimate additional corporate taxes. In fiscal 1972, State corporate taxes are estimated at $59.5 million, or $13 per capita. Thus, if 840 new Hollymead residents are migrants from other States, about $11,000 in State income taxes are likely to be generated regardless of any specific new commercial or industrial enterprises in Hollymead. However, many industrial facilities in the State export their products ,thus, their corporate taxes would not be directly related to increased demand for goods resulting from increased population or consumption.

An alternative method for approximating corporate taxes is to estimate additional employment likely to be created by the Hollymead commercial enterprises. Given that each net acre of commercial space results in 28.4 employees, 25 acres would employ 710 workers.[6] Since the State derives $53 per employee in the private sector in corporate taxes, over $37,000 would be obtained.

This approach has two major limitations. First, it is unlikely that the County can absorb 710 additional employees in retail or wholesale trade,

---

5. The income elasticity of these taxes is also assumed to follow the sales tax pattern.

6. The value of 28 employees per net acre has been derived by Fairfax County based on a three County surveys. See Fairfax County Division of Administrative Services, Projections of Employment and Related Uses in Fairfax County, Virginia, May 1972, p. 11.

since total employment in retail trades in 1970 was only 943.[7] Because of lower land values, commercial space may be used less intensively, reducing the number of employees per acre. Second, corporate tax revenues from comparatively low-wage labor intensive services are generally lower than taxes from capital intensive industrial enterprises; many retail stores are not even subject to corporate taxes. For purposes of this analysis, corporate taxes will be estimated conservatively at $15,000.

OTHER STATE REVENUES

The major State revenue sources, not part of the general fund, are the motor vehicle fuel tax and motor vehicle sales and registration tax, estimated to provide $195 million in fiscal 1972, or about $41 per capita. The amount of taxes collected from a jurisdiction depends on gallons of gasoline purchased, value of motor vehicles sold, and number of vehicles registered. Revenues are obtained from both households (private cars) and business enterprises (commercial vehicles). It can be assumed that receipts from Hollymead Phase I households should be at or slightly above the State average. The distribution of these funds is independent of collections.[8]

STATE EXPENDITURES

STATE EXPENDITURES BY FUNCTION

State expenditures can be grouped into two categories: (1) funds provided *directly* to local government, such as aid to elementary and

7. U.S. Bureau of the Census, *County Business Patterns--Virginia, 1970* (Washington, D.C.: U.S. Government Printing Office, 1971).

8. The County has approximately 0.40 vehicles per capita, the same as the State average.

secondary education, through categorical grants; and (2) services provided indirectly via State institutions and departments, such as higher education and welfare. Total general fund appropriations by function are shown in Table B-5.

TABLE B-5

General Fund Appropriations, 1971-1972*
(Categorical Grants)

Function	Percent of Total
Elementary-Secondary School Education	47.2
Higher and Other Education	16.3
Health and Welfare	17.1
Administration of Justice	6.8
Resource and Economic Development	2.6
General Administration	2.8
Other	7.2
TOTAL	100.0

*Division of the Budget, Analysis of Appropriations and Revenues 1970-1972 Biennum, Richmond, Va., December 1970.

STATE EXPENDITURES--CHANGES IN RESIDENCE

Intra-County migration has little, if any, impact on current expenditures, since major items, such as education, and health are not affected by such internal change in residence. By contrast, shifts from other areas of the County can have a considerable effect, particularly on the State cost of public education. For example, the State provided $228 in direct aid to the County per student in fiscal 1971. By contrast, the State provided $228 per student to two adjoining Counties--Green and Buckingham.[9] Thus, if a household with two children in public school moved from these areas to Albemarle, the State would save $120 for each year the children were attending public schools. Other services are less likely to be affected significantly by intra-State relocation.

Expenditures for residents from other states are sensitive to the demographic characteristics of in-migrants. Since education (both public schools and higher education) is a major component of the State budget, the likely utilization rate of schools determines, to a considerable degree, the cost of these households to the State. Except where in-migrants are indigent, social welfare costs are not affected by new households.

Capital expenditures which are partially or fully funded by the State can be effected by intra or inter-State migration. For example, the provision for facilities such as highways may increase in areas of rapid growth, while concurrently areas of out-migration (as many rural counties of the State) are likely to have capital facilities underutilized.

DIRECT STATE AID--HOLLYMEAD HOUSEHOLDS

The largest item in the State general fund for direct aid to local governments is public education, which represents 78.0 percent of the total local grant outlay. In 1971-1972, the State provided about $219 per student (ADM) from the general fund, in addition to state aid from sales tax redistribution.[10] In addition, about 13 percent of the amount distributed

9. Per student property value differences account for most of the State aid differential.

10. Supplementary State funds, derived by subtracting total cost of the minimum program from the local share ($.65 x 1970 market property value plus basic State share) are not provided to Albemarle County because of its relatively high property wealth. The addition of Hollymead Phase I will not effect the State aid distribution pattern.

directly is allocated for instructional staff retirement and social security.[11] Estimated State aid for education for households in Hollymead Phase I is contained in Table B-6.

TABLE B-6

State Aid for Public Education--
Hollymead Phase I Households

Dwelling Type	No. Students Per Unit	Direct State Aid	State Aid-Sales Tax	State Paid Benefits*	Total State Aid
Single Family	1.05	$233	$88	$30	$351
Townhouse	0.90	200	75	26	301
Apartment	0.43	95	36	12	143
Weighted Mean	0.85	$188	$71	$24	$283

*Includes social security, retirement, and life insurance.

WELFARE

With the exception of a small share of administrative costs, the State (and federal) government assumes the full cost of welfare in Virginia. In fiscal 1972, the State provided $877,754, or about $22 per capita, directly to the County to meet welfare costs. It is doubtful that the Hollymead Development will have any direct impact on the number of welfare recipients in the County. It could be argued that the secondary impact of the development, such as the expansion of labor employed by construction, would reduce the number of those on welfare, but this is speculative. Also, while the secondary effects of growth may result in the migration of low income families to the County, this too is speculative. It will be assumed that

---

11. These funds are not transferred directly to local jurisdictions.

the impact of the development with regard to welfare costs will be neutral--that is, State aid for welfare will not increase as a result of the new development.[12]

ABC PROFITS DISTRIBUTION

This per capita State aid is calculated at $11.50 for each Hollymead household.

CATEGORICAL GRANTS TO THE COUNTY

Categorical grants are made by the State to the County to provide services to both households and business enterprises. It is assumed that these categorical grants increase as a function of change in population and economic activity. It will be further assumed that 89 percent of the increase is due to population change, 11 percent to increased economic activity from new business enterprises.

OTHER DIRECT STATE GRANTS TO LOCAL GOVERNMENT

In addition to direct State grants which appear in the County budget, the State provides additional grants to local government. These include grants for planning, water quality control, and economic development. It will be assumed that an additional $3.00 per capita will be received for each Hollymead County resident for these services.

Table B-7 summarizes per capita non-education direct State aid to Albemarle County.

---

12. In 1971, Albemarle County had 0.63 percent of all welfare cases in the State; payments for recipients comprised 0.45 percent of the State total. Since the County comprises 0.81 percent of the State's population, the cost of welfare is below the State mean. See, Commonwealth of Virginia Department of Welfare, <u>Virginia Department of Welfare and Institutions</u>, June 1971, No. 4.

TABLE B-7

Non-Education Direct State Aid
to Albemarle County

Categorical Grant	Total	Household Allocation	Per Capita
Sheriff's Office (Public Safety)	$ 154,480	$ 137,487	$ 3.44
Finance Office (General Government)	108,983	96,995	2.42
Care of Prisoners	10,950	9,746	0.24
Administration of Justice	10,703	9,526	0.24
Welfare	877,754	22,250	21.94
Miscellaneous Grants	25,000	22,250	0.56
TOTAL	$1,187,870	$1,153,758	$28.84

Table B-8 summarizes total direct State aid to the County as a result of households in Hollymead Phase I.

TABLE B-8

Total Direct State Aid to Albemarle County--
Hollymead Phase I Households

Dwelling Type	Total Public Education Aid	Other State Programs	ABC Redistribution	TOTAL
Single Family	$351	$37	$13	$401
Townhouse	301	32	11	348
Apartment	143	26	9	178
Weighted Mean	$258	$33	$11	$327

INDIRECT STATE AID--HOLLYMEAD HOUSEHOLDS

The State of Virginia maintains a number of programs, such as higher education, which are administered directly by the State. Unless otherwise noted, programs which benefit both households and business enterprises will be allocated on the basis of commercial and business property in the State as a proportion of all real property. (In Virginia the share of industrial and commercial property is 22.3 percent of the total.)

HIGHER EDUCATION AND OTHER EDUCATIONAL UNITS

The total projected general revenues for the 1970-1972 biennum are $1,815 billion. Of this total, $1,042 billion, or 57.4 percent, is allocated in the form of aid received indirectly by jurisdictions from the State through State administered institutions.

The largest State-administered program is higher education, which received $278 million, or 16.0 percent of the general fund for the 1970-1972 time period.

Average State funds per student attending the University of Virginia are estimated at $1,800.[13] An examination of records indicates that in the fall of 1970, 267 students who are permanent residents of Albemarle County were attending the University of Virginia. In addition, 213 residents of Albemarle County attended other State-supported institutions in 1970, with an average cost to the State of approximately $1,400. In fiscal 1972, this enrollment from the County probably increased by 10 percent, or to a

13. Despite the high proportion of students from the County at the University, total enrollment in State institutions is only 50 percent of the expected total based on the County population. This may be due to the absence of community colleges (which account for 23 percent of total higher education enrollment) within the commuting distance and residents' high attendance rates at private universities.

total of about 530 students. The total cost to the State for all Albemarle County students is estimated at $778,800.[14]

In addition, the State supports associated educational units, such as two University hospitals, research institutions, and other facilities, whose total State allocation is estimated at $42 million for 1971-1972. Since Albemarle County residents utilize the University hospital more intensively than other State residents, the cost to the State for these associated educational units used by County residents is above the per capita State average of $9.

It will be assumed that these per capita expenditures are $18, or twice the State average. Thus, the total associated educational unit expenditure would be $720,000. Since Hollymead Phase I will contain 6.2 percent of the County population, about 33 students, or .04 per housing unit, could be expected to be at State institutions at a cost of $53,400.[15] In addition, the expenditures related to Hollymead Phase I for associated educational units, particularly the University hospital would total $44,600 per annum.

HEALTH PROGRAMS

State health programs include central administration activities, environmental sanitation, preventive medical services, and chronic disease control activities. These activities are estimated to total $11.3 million for 1971-1972, or about $2.50 per capita.

---

14. Data for students are from the State Council of Higher Education in Virginia, Report, Form R-1, which is submitted by each state-supported institution.

15. If in-migrant households are attracted to locate in the County because of the University of Virginia, the number may be higher. However, since the University is selective in its admissions policy, residence in the area does not assure admittance. Since the total number of students admitted appears not linked directly to the number of applicants, an increase in attendance from the County may not increase total State expenditures, although it may shift the permanent residence of certain students.

VOCATIONAL REHABILITATION

The total State expenditure for vocational rehabilitation in fiscal 1972 was $3 million from general funds, or less than $1.00 per capita; the major source of funds for this function is the federal government.

ADMINISTRATION OF JUSTICE

Approximately $61.5 million has been allocated for fiscal 1972 from general fund appropriations for the State Police, courts, and adult and juvenile correctional activities. Twenty-two percent of this will be allocated to business enterprises and 78 percent to households.

RESOURCE AND ECONOMIC DEVELOPMENT

Resource and economic development incorporates a broad spectrum of activities, including the State Departments of Agriculture, Labor and Industry, and Conservation, and the State Marine River Fisheries Division. Of the estimated $61 million appropriation, two-thirds will be allocated to business enterprises, one-third to households, since most of these functions primarily benefit commercial and industrial enterprises. Thus, $20.3 million, or $4.31 per capita, will be allocated to households in the State.

GENERAL ADMINISTRATION AND LEGISLATIVE

Included in the general administrative and legislative functions is the State Department of Taxation and Planning. The total cost for 1971-1972 is projected to be $29.5 million, of which 78 percent, or $23.0 million, will be allocated to households, the remainder to business enterprises.

STATE EMPLOYEE BENEFITS (Excluding Education)

This item totals $17.4 million; 90 percent will be allocated to households, 10 percent to business enterprises.

DEBT SERVICE AND OTHER FUNCTIONS

Debt service and miscellaneous functions total $23.6 million. Of this total, 90 percent will be allocated to households, 10 percent to business enterprises.

TOTAL INDIRECT STATE EXPENDITURES ALLOCATED TO HOLLYMEAD PHASE I HOUSEHOLDS (Except Education)

The total 1971-1972 cost of the above programs allocated to households is estimated at about $149 million, or $32 per capita, as shown in Table B-9.

TABLE B-9

Indirect State Aid to Albemarle County--
Hollymead Phase I Households*

Program	Total (In Millions)	Allocated to Households (In Millions)	Per Capita
Health Programs	$ 11.3	$ 11.3	$ 2.40
Vocational Rehabilitation	3.0	3.0	0.63
Administration of Justice	62.5	55.0	11.75
Resource and Economic Development	61.0	20.3	4.31
General Administration and Legislation	29.5	23.0	4.89
Employee Benefits	17.4	15.7	3.34
Debt Service and Other Functions	23.6	21.2	4.51
TOTAL	$208.3	$149.5	$31.83

*Excluding higher education.

OTHER STATE EXPENDITURES

The major expenditure which is not part of the general fund is transportation, primarily the construction and maintenance of highways. The allocation of State highway aid is based on a number of criteria only one of these being current population.[16] Since population is not the only factor considered by the State in the distribution of highway funds, in the short run additional demand for highways resulting from shifts in population primarily affect priorities in the selection of highway projects within the County with little change in total State expenditures. In the long run, total funds dispersed to the County are affected by population growth, but not in proportion to the additional population or tax revenues provided to the State as a result of growth.

In fiscal 1971, $1.5 million was allocated by the State to the primary road system in the County, or 0.8 percent of the total.[17] In addition, $1.2 million was allocated for the County's secondary roads in fiscal 1970.[18] Of secondary road funds, approximately one-half is appropriated for construction, the balance for road maintenance. It is crudely estimated that in fiscal 1971 the State spent about $70 per capita in highway funds.

The generally accepted method for estimating the effect of new residential and non-residential development on highway transportation is to calculate the number of car trips generated by the growth. This number is added to the existing traffic pattern to determine if the existing road system can absorb the additional cars without significantly reducing the

16. Other factors considered in allocating primary and secondary road systems include road mileage, vehicle miles traveled, and county area.

17. Commonwealth of Virginia Department of Highways, Primary System Allocation for Fiscal 1971, March 1971 (mimeo).

18. Commonwealth of Virginia Department of Highways, Secondary System Allocation, March 1969 (mimeo).

flow of traffic. Additional car trips, based on studies in various parts of Virginia, are contained in Table B-10.[19]

TABLE B-10

Estimated Car Trips--Hollymead Phase I Households

Dwelling Type	No. Units	No. Trips Per Day	Total Trips
Single Family	358	9	3,220
Townhouse	256	8	2,048
Apartment	197	7	1,393
TOTAL	813	24	6,666

The estimated total car trips generated by Hollymead households is close to the value derived by the County Planning Office. However, each 1,000 square feet of space in shopping centers generates an additional 45 trips per day. Since the number of square feet to be built on the 25 acres of net commercial space has not been estimated, the number of car trips cannot be approximated. However, if only 10 percent of the space (an extremely conservative value) is used for single story retail stores, this would result in about 117,000 square feet of space, or 5,265 car trips.

DIRECT AND INDIRECT STATE GRANTS--SUMMARY

Table B-11 shows the estimated total direct and indirect State grants to the County based on households in Hollymead Phase I.

19. Fairfax County Department of Administrative Services, Five-Year County Wide Development Program--Standards and Criteria, Vol. III, August 1972.

TABLE B-11

Total Direct and Indirect State Grants--
Hollymead Phase I Households

Dwelling Type	Direct Grants	Higher Education*	Other Direct Programs	TOTAL
Single Family	$401	$137	$118	$656
Townhouse	348	118	102	568
Apartment	178	96	83	357
Weighted Mean	$329	$121	$104	$554

*$98,000 allocated on a per capita basis, or $37 per capita. This includes the University hospital and related facilities.

STATE EXPENDITURES--HOLLYMEAD PHASE I BUSINESS ENTERPRISES

State expenditures for functions utilized by business enterprises include categorical grants to the County and State-administered programs. As shown in Table B-12, direct grants to Albemarle County, based on Hollymead Phase I total $34,112. These are allocated to the Hollymead commercial development in proportion to its share of the market value of all real property in the development or 11.7 percent.

TABLE B-12

Total Direct and Indirect State Grants--
Hollymead Phase I Business Enterprises

Type of Aid	State Expenditure	Allocation for Hollymead Business Enterprises
Direct County Aid	$34,112	$3,752
Total Indirect Aid	38,808	4,269
TOTAL	$72,920	$8,021

Indirect State programs utilized by business enterprises will be allocated to the County on the basis of employment in industrial and commercial enterprises in the County, which is 0.66 percent of the State total.

COMPARISON OF STATE REVENUES AND EXPENDITURES

A comparison of State revenues and expenditures (excluding highways) by dwelling type is shown in Table B-13.

TABLE B-13

Hollymead Phase I--Total State Revenues and Expenditures

Dwelling Type	Revenues	Expenditures	Surplus
Single Family	$919	$656	$263
Townhouse	635	568	67
Apartment	422	357	65
Weighted Mean	$706	$554	$152

As the Table B-13 indicates, the average household unit which inmigrates to Virginia yields a surplus to the State of $152. The surplus to the State is greatest in the case of higher income households in single family units. If, for example, all 813 Hollymead Phase I households were in-migrants to the State, the net annual revenue gain to the State would be $123,576, or in excess of the $101,745 annual County deficit.

Unfortunately, data on the likely proportion of in-migrants as a result of such a development are limited to Census estimates of all migrants to the County between 1965-1970. The use of these proportions indicates that it could be expected that about 31 percent of households in Hollymead Phase I will be new to Virginia. These families would provide net State surplus in excess of $38,000. In addition, business enterprises to be located in Hollymead Phase I will result in a net State surplus of about $7,000 per annum. Thus, the total State fiscal surplus as a result of Hollymead Phase I is likely to be approximately $45,000 per annum. Excluded from these calculations are increases in State revenues from households migrating within the State whose income changes as a result of moving to Albemarle County.

APPENDIX C
THE NET FISCAL IMPACT OF THE ENTIRE NORTH RIVANNA COMMUNITY CLUSTER ON ALBEMARLE COUNTY

When a large-scale development is proposed, such as the North Rivanna Community Cluster, it is frequently presented by the developers to local government officials in terms of a multi-phase project. Initially, approval may be requested for just the first subdivision which may represent only a fraction of the total development planned. In evaluating such a proposal, the fiscal impact of the total project on the local jurisdiction is seldom considered. This is particularly unfortunate if a local government grants approval for an initial section of a large project, because it is often difficult for it to then deny approval for subsequent sections, since large developers may argue that certain aspects of the initial section (e.g., roads, land for schools, the location of commercial facilities) are planned and based on the expectation of completing the entire development.

Thus, in considering the fiscal effect of one subdivision of a large development, such as Hollymead Phase I, attention should be paid to the potential impact the entire project will have on the local jurisdiction.

As noted in Chapter One, the entire North Rivanna Community Cluster, consisting of 3,510 acres, is envisioned to contain between 18,000 and 23,000 residents, equal to about half the present population of the County. The developer has provided the County with preliminary data on the first subdivision--Hollymead Phase I--including data on the distribution of acreage, and the density of residential units per acre. In its estimates, the County has assumed that the value of all residential units in the entire Cluster will be similar to values in Hollymead Phase I.

Further, it must be recognized that in view of increasing costs of labor and material, future construction, and thus real property value, is likely to be more expensive than present construction for similar units. Concurrently, on the basis of 1964-1972 trends for the County, as shown in Chapter Two, expenditures for public services can be expected to rise at a faster rate than revenues, necessitating tax increases. For the purposes of this analysis, it will be assumed that revenues will rise at the same rate as expenditures.

REVENUE ESTIMATES: NORTH RIVANNA COMMUNITY CLUSTER

Extrapolating from total per unit revenue data derived in Chapter Three for Hollymead Phase I, total revenues which will accrue to the County from households and business enterprises in the entire North Rivanna project are shown in Table C-1.

OPERATING AND CAPITAL EXPENDITURE ESTIMATES: NORTH RIVANNA COMMUNITY CLUSTER

Table C-2 contains estimates of both County operating and capital expenditures incurred by the North Rivanna Community Cluster. As with estimates of revenues, these calculations are based on expenditure data, by type of unit, derived for Hollymead Phase I in Chapters Four and Five.

The effect on capital costs (particularly for education) of the construction of a higher proportion of apartment units (two and three bedroom

TABLE C-1

Total Albemarle County Annual Revenues From Households and Business Enterprises in the North Rivanna Community Cluster[a]

Land-Use Type	No. of Acres	No. of Units	Revenue From Real Property[b] (in thousands)	Total From Cluster (in thousands)	% of Total From Cluster
Single Family	1,816[c]	2,419[d]	$ 678	$1,556	34.9
Townhouse		1,731	348	868	19.5
Apartment	145	2,900[e]	412	1,005	22.5
Commercial	110	N.A.	183	272	6.1
Industrial	423	N.A.	364	758	17.0
TOTAL	2,494	7,050	$1,985	$4,459	100.0

a. Data on acreage and number of units from Albemarle County Department of Planning, "Albemarle County Study of North Rivanna Cluster," 1972 (mimeo).

b. Revenue from commercial and industrial development based on Department of Planning estimates.

c. Allocation of acreage between single family and townhouses not specified.

d. Allocation between single family and townhouses based on Hollymead Phase I--58.3 percent single family, 41.7 percent townhouse.

e. Twenty units per acre.

units) in the entire Cluster than in Hollymead Phase I[1] is difficult to predict, especially since in many areas the supply of apartments already exceeds the demand. If, for instance, apartment rents do not increase as rapidly as the costs of residing in single family homes or townhouses, more households with school age children might remain in apartments. Therefore, this increased proportion of apartments might necessitate nearly the same capital expenditures as if more single family homes or townhouses were built.

---

1. Forty-one percent of the residential units in the entire North Rivanna Community Cluster will be apartments, while in the Hollymead Phase I, only 25 percent of residential units are apartments.

TABLE C-2

Total Albemarle County Annual Operating and Capital Expenditures for Households and Business Enterprises in the North Rivanna Community Cluster

Land-Use Type	No. of Units	Per Unit Operating Expenditure	North Rivanna-Linked Capital Cost Per Unit (30 Yr. Bonds)	Entire County-Linked Capital Cost Per Unit (30 Yr. Bonds)	Total Cost Per Unit	Total Expenditures for Cluster (in thousands)
Single Family	2,419	$597.89	$196.25	$74.98	$869.12	$2,102
Townhouse	1,731	512.11	168.22	64.85	745.18	1,290
Apartment	2,900	273.51	84.74	52.70	410.95	1,192
Commercial	N.A.	$43,802*	$3,266*	$17,830*	N.A.	$ 65
Industrial	N.A.	$86,792*	$6,434*	$35,557*	N.A.	$129

*Not on a per unit basis. Number represents total for all commercial or industrial.

With respect to operating expenditures for the Cluster, it should also be noted that since industrial parks are not planned until 1977-1978 phases of the development, there is likely to be a substantial lag between potential County revenues from industry and the need for expenditures, such as special fire protection equipment and sewerage facilities, to service these industries.

REVENUE-EXPENDITURE SUMMARY

The difference between revenues accruing to the County from the North Rivanna project and expenditures incurred by the entire development is shown in Table C-3. The estimated annual County deficit incurred by Cluster totals $253,000 as compared with $101,745 per annum for Hollymead. The annual mean per unit public sector deficit incurred by the entire Cluster ($50)

TABLE C-3

North Rivanna Community Cluster--Total Annual County Revenue-Expenditure Summary
(In Thousands)

Land-Use Type	Total County Revenues	Total County Expenditures (30-Year Bonds)	Difference Between Revenues and Expenditures
Single Family	$1,556	$2,102	-$546
Townhouse	868	1,290	- 422
Apartment	1,005	1,192	- 187
Commercial	272	65	+ 207
Industrial	758	129	+ 629
Subtotal	$4,459	$4,778	-$319
Less Existing Land Use	$ 34	N.A.	$ 34
TOTAL	$4,425	$4,778	-$353

is lower than the deficit resulting from Hollymead Phase I ($121). This is attributable to two factors: (1) the higher proportion of apartments in the entire Cluster than in Hollymead which suggests fewer school aged children and therefore lower expenditures for education; and (2) the inclusion of industrial development. This second factor is important because, although the real market value of business property as a proportion of the total market value of real property is the same in Hollymead Phase I as in the total Cluster,(about 22 percent), total revenues from business enterprises are higher in the Cluster because personal property taxes constitute about half of all local revenues per acre fron industrial facilities; the proportion for other business enterprises is much lower.

APPENDIX D
ESTIMATION OF EXPECTED SCHOOL ENROLLMENT BASED ON FERTILITY PROJECTIONS

An alternative approach for determining the number of students likely to attend public schools in the County as a result of the Hollymead Development is to estimate the number of children expected over a generation (30-33 years). While this approach has obvious limitations, in view of variations in migration patterns among jurisdictions, it provides an indirect method of estimating demand for school facilities.

Estimations can be made in the following manner. Since future birth rates are difficult to predict, any of three proxies may be utilized:

- The number of students per household based on the average fertility rate in Albemarle County in 1970 (3.1 children per woman ever married);
- The number of students based on 1971 Series D Census projections (2.5 children per woman);
- The number of students based on the total fertility rate for the nation in 1971, (2.3 children per woman).

In Albemarle County, approximately 92 percent of all school-age children are enrolled in public schools. In view of recent national demographic patterns, a range between 2.3 and 2.5 children per household appears realistic for long range planning. Therefore, since the average student from a middle-income household will spend 12.5 (K-12) years in public school, regardless of the type of housing, the number of school years per household will vary from 26.5 to 28.2.

That is, if the demographic pattern in Albemarle County does not deviate from the nation, between 0.80 and 0.85 children can be expected from each household over a generation (33 years). This value closely approximates the average for each Hollymead unit determined from the County Planning Department surveys.

From a planning viewpoint, this long-range approach to estimating number of students has limitations, since most households have more than one student in public schools concurrently, preceded and followed by a period when there are no school-age children in the household. Since households residing in rental units tend to be younger, they are more likely to require elementary schools, while those residing in middle-income single family units tend to be older and have children of high-school age. In addition, migration patterns differ among jurisdictions--suburbs tend to have more households with school-age children compared to central cities. Finally, factors such as racial distribution and regional factors affect demographic patterns.

APPENDIX E
ESTIMATION OF CAPITAL EXPENDITURES BASED ON THE COUNTY'S PROJECTED CAPITAL IMPROVEMENT PROGRAM

A way of estimating the capital needs of the County as a result of development is to examine the proposed capital improvements program for the County.[1] The County report recommends a number of projects to be undertaken in the next five years. Beyond the five-year period, capital needs are discussed in general terms. Of primary interest for this study are: (1) projects not likely to be financed through general obligation revenue bonds; and (2) the County cost of projects whose total cost is shared by the State or federal agencies. Primary and secondary schools are excluded.

TABLE E-1

Proposed Capital Projects for Albemarle County*

Water Supply Sources (1972-1975)	$2,545,867
Refuse Disposal (1972-1973)	100,000
Community College (1971-1972)	1,000,000
Vocational Training (1972-1973)	1,300,000
Detention Facility (1972-1973)	1,500,000
Airport Control Tower (1971-1972)	200,000
TOTAL	$6,645,867

*Recreation facilities budgeted in 1971-72 have been omitted.

---

1. R. H. Payne, Capital Improvement Program, Albemarle County, 1970 - 200, March 1971.

The proposed projects in these categories are shown in Table E-1.

Partial funding for certain projects has been initiated in fiscal 1972. The average annual expenditures for the projects shown in Table B-1 over a five-year period is approximately $1.3 million if the above projects are representative. However, the issuance of a 20 or 30-year bond will not be sufficient to meet the capital needs of the County over an extended time period. Presumably an additional $6.6 million (in constant dollars and population) will be needed in 1977 to meet capital expenditures for the following five-year interval.

The proposed capital improvement program is insufficient for long-term planning, since the assumptions regarding inflation and demography, as well as socioeconomic characteristics and size of future population, are not stated. However, the plan suggests that capital needs to be met from current revenues in the next decade will average approximatley over $1.3 million annually. Again, this amount excludes public schools and projects to be financed through general revenue bonds.

APPENDIX F
ADDITIONAL FACTORS TO BE EXAMINED

ECONOMIC FACTORS

Because of the limited nature of this study the fiscal analysis does not include all the relevant economic factors which should be considered in determining the economic impact of new developments. A number of these factors are noted below:

Change in Value of Adjacent Land. In general, residential construction in a previously undeveloped area increases the value of surrounding land. If the land remains undeveloped, but its assessed value is increased by the jurisdiction, there is a fiscal gain in the form of higher property tax receipts to the county. However, this increase in value is due primarily to the anticipation of future development. Once such development takes place, the fiscal impact cannot be projected *a priori*. If future development is constrained by the county, the value of adjacent land will not be significantly altered from its present level. However, increases in land value in one area may be offset by decreases in other areas resulting from the locational shift in the demand for land.

Land Donated by Developer. Frequently developers of a large area provide land for schools, recreation, and other facilities. In this situation, the annualized net value of the land, determined by the price the jurisdiction would have to pay for similar land, has to be included in the fiscal analysis. In the Albemarle County study, for example, the cost for an elementary school was adjusted to reflect the donation of land by the developer. Facilities not usually provided by the jurisdiction (such as a private golf course) should not be considered a benefit to the total community, but rather as an asset to those purchasing property in the development.

Lag Between Revenues and Expenditures. In most cases, there is a lag between revenues accruing to a jurisdiction from new development and expenditures incurred by new residents. This is due, in part, to the necessity of providing part of the infrastructure (as roads, utilities) prior to private development. In addition, the construction time for public facilities (such as schools) is generally longer than for residential units. Therefore, a precise analysis should include the additional interim tax burden on the existing taxpayers while the development and the capital facilities are under construction.

Impact on Employment. In communities where there is an employment shortage among construction workers, a new development provides at least short-term employment; this is likely to have a positive fiscal impact on the public sector. However, most persons unemployed during periods of national expansion are unskilled, and not likely to be employed as a result of construction activity; thus, an increase in construction activity may attract persons from outside the jurisdiction, without necessarily benefiting those who lack employment in the community.

Commercial development is likely to generate additional employment in retail trades. It is not feasible, however, to estimate what jobs will be taken by present county residents, person commuting to a county from other jurisdictions, or those who will migrate to a county as a result of the expansion in employment.

PHYSICAL ENVIRONMENT

The impact of population and industrial growth on all forms of pollution --water, air, noise--has been the subject of considerable discussion.[1] The effect of additional people and industrial activity on the environment is extremely area-sensitive. That is, conditions particular to a given location determine the impact of increased economic activity on the incremental level of pollution. Thus, these factors must be taken into account in analyzing development plans.

OTHER FACTORS

Factors which need to be considered in evaluating the impact of new development include aesthetics, cultural values, health and safety, recreation, education, local transportation, housing, and social conditions. A discussion of the methods for measuring these factors can be found in a recent report by the Urban Institute on land use changes.[2]

---

1. See, for example, W. A. Johnson and J. Hardesty, Eds., _Economic Growth vs. the Environment_ (Belmont, Calif.: Wadsworth Publishing Company, 1971).

2. P. Schaenman, T. Muller, J. Kalish, D. Talbott, "Measuring for Evaluating Land Development," The Urban Institute, September 1972.

APPENDIX G
DATA SOURCES FOR A FISCAL IMPACT ANALYSIS

Following is a summary of suggested sources of data needed to estimate the fiscal impact of new residential and non-residential development. It is in no way intended to be an exhaustive listing, but is primarily to serve as a general guide for use in examining the fiscal impact of growth at the County level.

RESIDENTIAL DEVELOPMENT-REVENUE ESTIMATES

LOCAL REAL PROPERTY TAX REVENUES

These revenues may be calculated by multiplying the estimated market (real) value of new real property by the effective tax rate, deducting exemptions such as homestead, old age-low income, veteran status, etc.[1] The effective tax rate for a new development is usually not what the community utilizes as its market-to-assessment ratio guide, but rather has to be determined by comparing the market value of current sales to actual residential assessment. This value is, in almost all cases, lower than the "official" market-to-assessed ratio, particularly in an inflationary period, when there is a lag between the nominal assessed value and actual assessed value.[2]

---

1. For a discussion of Property tax exemptions, by area, see R. W. Lindholm, ed., Property Taxation U.S.A. (Madison, Wisc.: University of Wisconsin Press, 1969).

2. For effective tax rates by land-use category and county, see U.S. Bureau of the Census, 1967 Census of Government-Taxable Property Value, Vol. II (Washington, D.C.: U.S. Government Printing Office, October 1968).

Thus, the use of "official assessment ratios tends to exaggerate property tax collections.

For income-producing property (such as a large apartment building), property taxes may not be based on the value of the building, but rather on a share of gross income or net profits. This assessment approach can result in higher revenues compared to taxes based on the value of the building, unless many units are not occupied.

PERSONAL PROPERTY AND SALES TAXES

These taxes require the estimation of the anticipated income of new households. Income data may be calculated from Census or other data for areas of comparable housing or by the indirect approach which is discussed in Chapter Three of the case study.

Personal property subject to taxation varies widely among states and jurisdictions.[3] The most common items subject to this tax are automobiles, boats, and to a lesser extent, household goods. The value of these can be estimated by their relation to income. In the case of automobiles, it is necessary to determine which method is used as a basis for calculating their value (as wholesale price, loan value, market price) and the effective tax rate.

Estimated sales tax receipts should be based on the purchasing patterns of similar households in the region.[4] The average household size can be

---

3. Characteristics of local and state taxes are discussed in Advisory Commission on Intergovernmental Relations, State-Local Finances: Significant Features and Suggested Legislation (Washington, D.C.: U.S. Government Printing Office, 1972).

4. Regional data on consumer expenditures by size of household can be found in U.S. Department of Labor, Bureau of Labor Statistics, Survey of Consumer Expenditures (Washington, D.C.: U.S. Government Printing Office, 1964).

estimated by the type of housing unit from U.S. Census of Housing statistics (e.g., single family homes have generally more persons with higher median ages compared to apartments). The fraction of purchases subject to sales tax made within the jurisdiction can be estimated by comparing per capita sales tax receipts in the jurisdiction with others within commuting distance, adjusted for differences in income.

UTILITY TAXES

Utility taxes are frequently levied as a percentage of utility bills. Estimates of average bills can be based on utilities' data for various types of residences (such as large single family dwellings, smaller single family dwellings, apartments).

OTHER LOCAL TAXES

Other local taxes may have to be estimated, including cigarette taxes, car registration fees and local income tax surtaxes, and local payroll taxes. In addition, business enterprises are subject to local license fees, permits and other charges which also must be approximated.

TAXES FROM PREVIOUS LAND USE

The taxes collected for the previous land use should be estimated and subtracted from the anticipated revenues to determine the net change in revenues. If the residents or businesses displaced by the development leave the jurisdiction, estimates of property and other tax revenues lost (as well as expenditures reduced) may be needed.

RESIDENTIAL DEVELOPMENT--OPERATING EXPENDITURES

EDUCATION

The number of students anticipated from residential development can be estimated based on the type of housing and demographic characteristics of the jurisdiction. For example, single family homes tend to have more school age students compared to apartments. Multi-bedroom units have more students than single bedroom apartments, and "luxury" high-rise apartments tend to have very few public school students. Estimates of the average number of students per type of housing unit for each level of school are generally available from the local board of education. Other factors to be considered include income (e.g., high income families are more likely to send their children to private school); and ethnic factors (e.g., Spanish-speaking Americans and blacks have higher birthrates than whites).[5] Also, suburban areas tend to have more households with school-age children than do central cities.

NON-EDUCATION OPERATING EXPENDITURES

Non-education operating costs can be roughly estimated by utilizing established standards based on population density; for example, the ratio of nine hospital beds per 1,000 population and 1.5 police per 1,000 population, etc.[6] Given the cost per policeman or hospital bed, operating cost

5. See U.S. Bureau of the Census, 1970 Census of Population, General Population Characteristics, PC(1)B (Washington, D.C.: U.S. Government Printing Office, 1972), for fertility rates by race for urban and rural areas of each state.

6. For discussion of criteria for fire protection, police protection, recreation and health services as a function of population, see Five Year Countywide Development Program-Standards and Criteria, Vol. III, Fairfax County Department of Administrative Services.

for each increment in population can be calculated.[7] Other services, such as fire protection, are linked to both area and population density.[8]

RESIDENTIAL DEVELOPMENT--CAPITAL EXPENDITURES

Most jurisdictions have capital improvement plans which project the need for new public services, and estimate the cost of providing new facilities. In the absence of additional data, capital expenditures should be allocated to new households on a per capita basis.[9]

Cost for existing facilities to be used by the development must be partially allocated to the developement if such use will result in the need for facility expansion. Therefore, key data items to be obtained are the degree to which existing facilities are being utilized. For example, one should determine existing classroom space available to the development, how many more police can be accommodated in existing structures, and how much additional sewerage can existing plants treat without degradation in treatment quality. In the case of fire protection, even a comparatively small development, more than two or three miles distance from an existing fire company, is likely to require a new facility in order for the residents to maintain standard insurance rates.

---

7. This simplified approach assumes that there are no economies or diseconomies of scale associated with expanding services, and that, the characteristics of the new population do not deviate from the present population.

8. For a discussion of public service financing, see W. S. Vickrey, "General and Specific Financing of Public Services," in Public Expenditure Decision in the Urban Community, H. G. Schaller, ed. (Washington, D.C.: Resources for the Future, 1963).

9. Total per annum amortized expenditures for each function divided by present population. Amortization should be based on current bond interest rate and the length of the bonds to be issued (i.e., 20-year or 30-year bonds).

It is also useful to determine at what increments in population or demand has the decision has been made to expand capital facilities in the past. Since the demand for facilities is linked to such factors as household density and income, data gathered to estimate operating expenditures is also useful in estimating the demand for new facilities.

NON-RESIDENTIAL DEVELOPMENT

Non-residential development includes both commercial (e.g., retail trade, office buildings, etc.) and industrial enterprises. The fiscal evaluation of commercial and industrial development is more complex than for residential development since: (1) less data are usually available on the characteristics of non-residential development from zoning applications; (2) the secondary impact of non-residential development, namely inmigration, must be considered; and (3) non-residential development may cause considerable spill-over effects on nearby jurisdictions.

Frequently the only data provided are that a commercial development (e.g., a shopping center) or an industrial park is to be built on a certain site and will occupy a given number of acres. The developer may not know what specific enterprises will locate, although potential occupants are usually solicited prior to the land-use change. However, to determine the fiscal impact of non-residential development it is necessary to roughly estimate the number, wage structure, and residence of new employees.

Several approaches can be utilized to approximate the number and type of employment and local revenues generated by new industrial-commercial activity. If only the number of acres to be utilized is provided, ratios can be used which have been developed nationally for estimating the number and type of employees required by various types of business activity.[10] For example, for retail trade and personal services, 380 square feet per employee of enclosed space are required, with a building covering 25 percent of the total land area. In construction, transportation and public utilities, one acre per 10 employees is needed; for research and technical manufacturing, one acre per 40 employees; and for other industrial uses, one acre per 15 employees.[11] Floor space per employee in service industries has been calculated for suburban areas.[12]

Primary employment (such as manufacturing) requires other workers to provide support services within commuting distance of the new development.[13] For example, 43 retail trade workers are employed in Virginia for each 1,000 inhabitants. Thus, 3,000 new residential residents are likely to result in a secondary demand for 129 retail trades workers.

If the specific type of industry or commercial enterprise to be located in a community is known, average wages (for production and non-production labor) can be estimated for the SMSA or the county from such Census Bureau documents as the Census of Manufacturers, and County Business Patterns. Employees' characteristics for a specific industry can be estimated from special surveys conducted by the Department of Labor and industry associations. In most cases, the business enterprise which is to build a facility has considerable data on the occupation type and wage distribution of its

---

10. Fairfax County Division of Administrative Services, Projections of Employment and Related Uses in Fairfax County, Virginia, May 1972.

11. Maryland-National Capital Park and Planning Commission, Commercial Land Use in Montgomery and Prince George's Counties, May 1959.

12. Urban Land Institute, The Dollars and Cents of Shopping Centers (Washington, D.C.: Urban Land Institute, 1966).

13. U.S. Bureau of the Census, 1970 County Business Patterns, (CBP-70-1) (Washington, D.C.: U.S. Government Printing Office, 1971).

labor force. In general, organizations survey the availability of labor prior to determining the location of new facilities.

DATA ON OTHER FACTORS

In addition to estimating the number and residence of new employees resulting from non-residential development, two additional factors should be noted: the secondary impact of non-residential development (i.e., inmigration of new employees) and spill-over effects of development to neighboring jurisdictions. Both of these factors are complex, and data for estimating their fiscal impact are difficult if not impossible to obtain, since most often, the developer is not required to provide information about the kind of industrial or commercial development which is to be located in an anticipated industrial park or shopping center. Although this is often the case, secondary impact and spill-over effects should not be ignored.